THE HUMAN ENTREPRENEUR

The Human Entrepreneur

Find Your Authentic Voice, Start Your Business, & Craft Your Legacy

Marawan Nassar

Award-Winning Entrepreneur & Mentor

Published by Game Changer Publishing

Paperback ISBN: 978-1-965653-99-9

Hardcover ISBN: 978-1-965653-07-4

Digital ISBN: 978-1-965653-08-1

www.GameChangerPublishing.com

DEDICATION

To all aspiring entrepreneurs and seekers of authenticity, this book is for you. Also, it's dedicated to my wife and our children, Raheem and Dima, who inspire everything I do. May this guide help you discover your true self and create a meaningful impact and life. Let's uphold the values of giving, loving, and thriving as we build lives and businesses that truly matter.

Read This First

Just to say thanks for buying and reading my book, I would like to give you a free welcome call with me, no strings attached!

Scan the QR Code Here:

SCAN ME

The Human Entrepreneur

Find Your Authentic Voice, Start Your Business, & Craft Your Legacy

Marawan Nassar

GAME CHANGER PUBLISHING

www.GameChangerPublishing.com

In a world often driven by the relentless pursuit of profit, Marawan stands as a beacon of authenticity and purpose. His unique approach to entrepreneurship is not merely about building successful businesses; it's about crafting ventures that are deeply rooted in positive psychology and genuine human values.

As someone who knows Marawan personally, I have witnessed firsthand his unwavering commitment to helping others discover their true potential and achieve their dreams.

The Human Entrepreneur is more than just a book; it is a reflection of its author's life and philosophy. Marawan combines a keen business acumen with an insightful understanding of the human psyche, creating a holistic model that is both innovative and inspiring. His methods do not just teach you how to start a business; they guide you on how to build something that is meaningful, impactful, and sustainable.

What sets Marawan apart is his authenticity. In an era where success is often equated with compromise, Marawan proves that it is possible to achieve greatness without losing one's integrity. His teachings are grounded in real-world experience and a genuine desire to make a positive difference.

This book is a valuable read for anyone looking to embark on a journey of growth, innovation, and true success.

-Ashraf Helal
Management consultant, MCC leadership coach and author

* * *

Giving, as one of life's core values, is beautifully encapsulated by Marawan Nassar: "Giving is what makes you alive, what makes you tick, what makes life fulfilling." His commitment to giving began during his undergraduate years, marking the start of a long and impactful journey as a mentor.

With a background in petroleum exploration, Marawan draws parallels between drilling deep for hydrocarbons and delving into the depths of our minds to uplift our brand and reach the Giver stage. He continually encourages people to identify their values, understand their strengths, and pursue their passions.

-Samir Abdelmoaty
Chairman of the Egyptian Geophysical Society

Foreword

I met Marawan when he completed our Diploma of Positive Psychology and Wellbeing in 2016. From the moment we connected, I could see his deep passion for learning and personal growth.

Marawan has always been driven by a desire to make a difference—in his own life and the lives of others. This passion has shaped his journey as a leader and an entrepreneur, which is beautifully captured in *The Human Entrepreneur.*

This book is more than just a guide for business owners; it's about the human side of entrepreneurship. In today's world, it's easy to get caught up in the rush to succeed, focusing only on profits, growth, and competition. Marawan reminds us that being an entrepreneur is also about connecting with who we are as people—our strengths, our values, and our wellbeing. He weaves in ideas from positive psychology, showing how building a business can be a meaningful and fulfilling journey and a financial one.

Marawan shares his deeply personal and authentic journey from his personal near-death experience, which prompted him to confront his fears, particularly the fear of judgment, which had been holding him back from sharing his voice and wisdom. After this experience, he changed his life by studying happiness and fulfilment through positive psychology. This journey led him to become a positive psychology practitioner and eventually start a business focused on blending success with fulfilment.

This book takes the reader on their own journey through the Identity Brand Cycle to create an entrepreneurial mindset based on personal values, strengths and passions to inform their future. There are tangible ideas around trends, career progression, decision-making in business, and how to create your personal story. Readers can follow along, seeing and experiencing their personal and professional growth as they turn the pages.

At a time when the world is changing faster than ever, *The Human Entrepreneur* offers a fresh perspective on how we can lead with purpose, balance work with personal wellbeing, and create businesses that reflect our core values. It's a reminder that success doesn't have to come at the cost of our happiness or health. This book shows us how to bring our whole selves into our work—how to be successful entrepreneurs while staying true to who we are as human beings.

In these pages, you will find real stories, practical tips, and powerful tools that will help you navigate the challenges of entrepreneurship with a human-centred approach. Whether you are starting out or have been running a business for years, Marawan's insights will inspire you to rethink what it means to be a successful entrepreneur today.

I am incredibly proud of Marawan and the journey he has taken since we first met. His dedication to his personal growth and professional life is truly admirable. *The Human Entrepreneur* is a testament to that journey, and I know it will bring immense value to anyone who reads it.

– Sue Langley, CEO and Founder of the Langley Group

Table of Contents

INTRODUCTION

The Spark: The Accidental Entrepreneur

"What you seek is seeking you."
– Rumi, Persian poet and Islamic scholar

My wife and I were on a plane, traveling to Sharm El-Sheikh, one of the resorts on the Red Sea in Egypt. It would be our first time visiting the resort. The weather was nice, and we were enjoying ourselves immensely. But then something happened. While we were in the air, the plane started to shake. My wife and I grew frightened. We didn't know what was going on. The turbulence became so rough that people began to scream.

A single thought ran through my mind: *This is the end.*

I had built a successful career with a master's in applied geology. I drove an expensive car, owned a large home, and had a beautiful wife. Despite my success, I was not fulfilled. My dream was to add value to the world. My dream was to leave a legacy. My dream was to share my wisdom and insight with others. But I hadn't done any of those things. I realized this was not because I didn't have the knowledge but because I was afraid. I was afraid to let my voice go out. I was afraid of other people's judgment. Because of that fear, I couldn't be myself. I couldn't share my voice. Then, I realized that my biggest fear was fear itself.

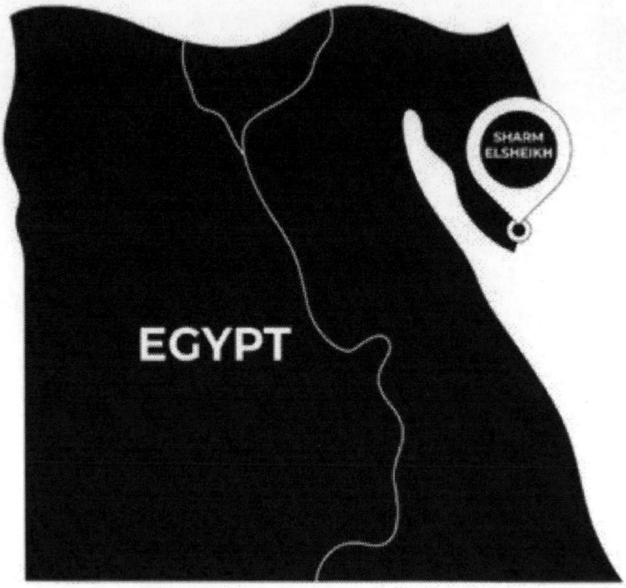

The turbulence continued for a few minutes. The situation was not easy for us passengers, but the captain said that the plane had hit a thunderstorm and he needed to maneuver around it. Finally, we landed at Sharm El Sheikh International Airport, safe and sound, but I was a different person with a new perspective. I had decided to change my life. From that point on, I would study happiness and fulfillment.

I'm a scientist, so I need to have everything explained by science. This is why I decided to study positive psychology—it's the closest field to the study of happiness and fulfillment. I found that success is entirely different from happiness, and both may have different paths.

I traveled to London, where I studied positive psychology with one of my mentors, Sue Langley, and became a positive psychology practitioner. I started to see the world from a different perspective. I'm sometimes still afraid or worried, but those feelings do not hold me back from achieving my dreams any more.

After this journey of searching to understand what happiness and fulfillment are, I wanted to do something with what I had learned. So, I started sharing my thoughts about how to mix success and fulfillment with the people in my life, friends and family, who were saying to me, "We, too, would like to shift our careers. How can we do that? And if we change our careers, will we find happiness? Will we find fulfillment?"

I began to share what I had learned on my journey. I held workshops and webinars and soon discovered that I had accidentally started a business. While I had taken many courses on business, I hadn't studied it at university. As I learned more about how to create and grow a business, I found that, yes, your company has a body, but you also need to give it a soul. You need to give it a spirit.

This discovery led me to talk more about becoming a **Human Entrepreneur**. How can you be yourself? How can you embody your emotions, spirit, values, and strengths? When you do that, you will not only be successful but also live a fulfilled life. Whether you're an employee or an entrepreneur, it doesn't matter. What matters is being a human first before being an entrepreneur or an employee. This is what I decided to share with the world.

Yes, you can be a successful employee or a successful entrepreneur, but sometimes, more is needed. You need to feel the success from the inside out. You need to feel the fulfillment from the inside out. It is only possible to do that if you understand your motivations, your values, your why, and your purpose. I know those are big words, but sometimes, big words have meanings that can guide us. I know you can feel it. Maybe it's not a meaning. Maybe it's an identity, a brand, or a destination. It doesn't matter what the word itself is; what matters is how you feel. Do you feel fulfilled or not?

I'm still on my journey from success to fulfillment. I'm still figuring it out, and I'm still exploring because, every day, when I talk about success, I match it with fulfillment. When I achieve something, I align it with fulfillment and happiness.

Discovering the IdentityBrand Cycle

I used my experience to develop a process on how to become a **Human Entrepreneur**—how to be yourself, build a sustainable business in one cycle, and lead a business that resonates with your deep *why* yet still attracts and converts customers and clients. I call it the **IdentityBrand Cycle**.

When I studied psychology and geology, I found that the two are related.

For example, we go through a cycle when we search for oil and gas resources. This cycle starts with uncovering. We determine the company's objective, what we are looking for, and our overall strategy. Next, we explore, finding out which companies have worked in the area before and what they discovered. Was it oil, gas, gold, or nothing? Third, we define. After exploring the area of interest, we identify where we need to drill. Then, we design the drill bit and gather the resources we need to drill at that specific location. Every layer of rock has unique characteristics, with different pressures and temperatures. Some rocks are solid, and some rocks are soft. We must design the well based on what we know about the subsurface. If we don't, disasters can happen while drilling.

After that, we act—in this case, we start to drill. But it's a cycle. Sometimes, when we drill, we succeed and find exactly what we aim for, and sometimes, we don't. The cycle doesn't stop because we take this success or failure and embed it in the cycle itself. Maybe we need to have a different objective based on new information. Maybe we need to explore more. Maybe we need to identify another location to drill. Maybe we need to design our well better. Maybe we need to act differently. And the cycle goes on and on.

When I started a business, I found that entrepreneurs follow the same cycle. For example, before starting our business, we need to uncover who we are, why we want to start our own business, what the driver is, and what will motivate us to continue. After that, we need to explore or do market research. What kind of products or services are other people providing? What are the benefits? What are they doing well, and what can they improve? Next, we need to define our values and who we want our customers to be. Then, we need to design and create products that fit our customer's needs and develop ways to deliver them. Finally, we need to act, which means doing things like marketing, publishing, and posting on social media. When you act, because the process is a cycle, you uncover new things about yourself. You explore as well, leading you to define and design different products, and the cycle continues.

The difference between the cycles in oil and gas and entrepreneurship is the pyramid inside each. When we move through the entrepreneurship cycle, we are building a unique mindset from the bottom up.

Most entrepreneurs need to be influencers. They need to leave a legacy behind, but this is actually the top of the pyramid. The pyramid consists of five stages. To become a giver, you need to fulfill four different levels first.

1. **The Dreamer:** The dreamer is a person who has a dream, a burning desire to achieve something. But dreams are not enough. You need to build on your dream. To do this, you must become a planner.
2. **The Planner:** The planner is someone who plans for the dream. They perform tasks, have responsibilities, and build habits to achieve their dreams. However, more than having a dream and a plan, you need to be influential and leave a legacy.
3. **The Marketer:** You also need to have a marketer's mindset. Marketing is not a skill. Marketing is a mindset. We do marketing every day. We do marketing with our kids. We do marketing in our jobs. We do marketing when we buy things. We do marketing when we sell things. Marketing is a life skill, a mindset. Who else has the same heart as you? You need to be the best marketer because you will use this mindset to influence your employees and customers. Who else will communicate your message with your heart? That's why having the mindset of a marketer is so important for fulfilling your dream. So, you cannot be an influencer if you are a dreamer without a plan. And being a planner is not enough to be an influencer. You need to market your dream. After going through the cycle several times, the next mindset you need to adopt is that of a CEO.
4. **The CEO:** Being a CEO is all about effective management. Whether you have employees, customers, influencers, or followers, you have to handle it all. Adopting the CEO mindset and taking responsibility makes progressing to the next level and becoming a giver easier.
5. **The Giver:** Some may call this being an influencer, but I prefer to call it being a giver, as your focus at this stage should be solely on giving, not seeking anything in return. Giving is what makes you alive. Giving is what makes you tick. Giving is what makes life fulfilling.

When you go through this cycle many times, you start to balance your mindset from the bottom to the top, from the dreamer to the planner to the marketer to the CEO to the giver. At that moment, you will discover that you are a giver from the inside out. This will give you not only the motivation to build a business and serve people but also to be close to who you are and the happiness you are looking for. So, this is the pyramid, and this is the cycle. In this book, we will discuss in depth how to build a business that leads to success and fulfillment.

Entrepreneurship Is a Mindset, Not a Title

In today's rapidly changing world, the entrepreneurial mindset is no longer exclusive to business owners and startups. Whether you are an employee, business owner, or even a parent, cultivating an entrepreneurial mindset has become essential for personal and professional growth.

It's not a title; it's a mindset. Focusing on an entrepreneurial mindset will empower you to inspire others and live the life you want. You will not be looking to change your role from parent, business owner, or startup founder; your entrepreneurial mindset will make you a different person.

On my journey, many of the people I encountered were simply pursuing a title. When they got it, they were often not ready for it. This made them hate the title—and sometimes, they even hated themselves. Similarly, people often compare themselves to others and compete with them. By doing this, they only put pressure on themselves.

After working with two thousand entrepreneurs from all over the world and from different industries, I discovered that everyone has a different growth rate. Sometimes, we need to respect our rate. Look at the flowers around you. Look at the trees. They all have different traits and growth rates, and they all have different beauty as well.

In the next few chapters, we will discuss what it means to be a **Human Entrepreneur**. It's not just about building a business. It's about finding a guiding force to drive your business that makes you who you are so that when you leave this planet, you won't regret it.

When I was on the plane, the pain of regret was much more powerful than the fear I felt. I regretted that I didn't go further because of my fear. I regretted refusing to be on a stage because of my fear. Try to live every moment from now on. Don't just build a business; build a heart that can accommodate both success and fulfillment.

CHAPTER 1

Uncover: Uplift Your True Identity

"The privilege of a lifetime is to become who you truly are."
– Carl Jung, the "Father" of analytical psychology

I have spoken with many people who are interested in changing their careers, either because they are dissatisfied with their current job or because they get bored easily and want to try something new. Regardless of the reason, the common goal is to find fulfillment in their work.

To make informed decisions about your career path, it is important first to understand who you are and what you want. This involves asking questions like why you want to switch careers, where you want to go, and what you hope to gain from the change. Similarly, if you frequently get bored with your work, you should reflect on why that is and what would make a new job or location more interesting to you. By taking the time to understand your motivations and priorities, you can make choices that are more likely to lead to long-term satisfaction and avoid regretting your decisions down the line.

Sometimes, our boats move from one body of water to another—from the Red Sea to the Mediterranean and from the Mediterranean to the Atlantic Ocean. However, sometimes, the issue is not with the sea or the ocean but with the boat itself. If the boat is leaking, it will sink wherever it is placed. This is why we need to think about ourselves as the boat. We need to ensure that we are not leaking and are in good condition to sail through life smoothly.

Growing up, one of the most influential things in my life was the stories my father told me. Even though he passed away when I was almost 18, the memories of those stories continue to shape my personality to this day.

One story he told repeatedly was about the scientists of Andalusia during the golden age of Islam. He talked about geniuses like Ibn Rushd and Ibn Sina, who excelled in many different fields, such as philosophy, medicine, law, and mathematics. I was fascinated by how they could master so many different sciences and skills.

Reflecting on those stories still motivates me to explore different fields and seek meaning in learning and mastering new skills. As I grew up, I realized that there is a deeper meaning behind the stories. During that time, these Islamic scientists pursued different fields not just because they liked them but because the fields were a part of their identity or would help them reach their identity.

I began to question what my true identity was and how I could discover it. Was it as simple as reading a book or taking a course? As someone with a scientific mind, I needed something concrete to build on. After much reflection,

I found that three things have helped me craft my identity and make decisions in my life: Values, Strengths, and Passions, or VSP.

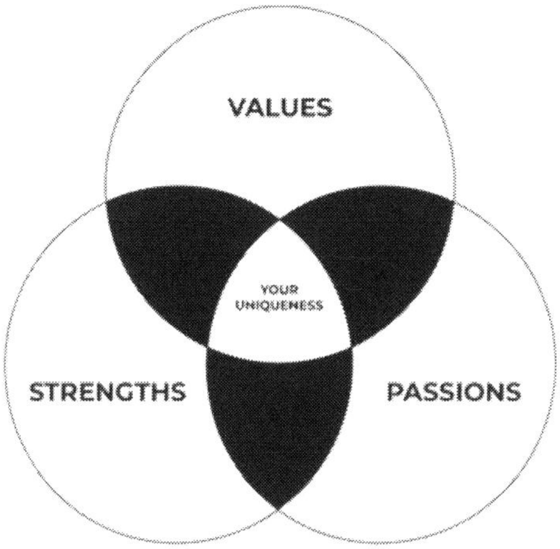

However, it's not just about the three words but the harmony between them. While working as a geologist, I discovered something called a VSP or Vertical Seismic Profile. This helps in studying the earth's internal structure, revealing different layers with different physical properties. It's a scientific method for understanding the earth and the subsurface so that we know where to drill and what we are drilling through.

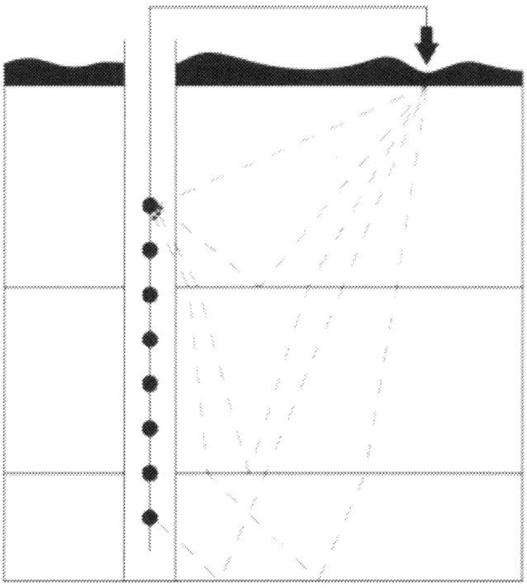

I found a match between the VSP of geology and the VSP of life. Without our personal VSP, we don't know why we need to make certain decisions. For example, why should we pursue entrepreneurship, and why not? Why should we pursue a career in a particular field, and why not? Finding harmony between our values, strengths, and passions is crucial. They can be our guiding force for every decision we make, especially when building a business.

The following steps will help you not only identify and understand your values, strengths, and passions but also how to link them together to find harmony. This will help you make better decisions and guide you toward fulfilling your true identity.

Uncover Your Values

Values refer to the emotional states that we believe are significant to experience or avoid in our careers and lives. According to most studies, the foundation of core values is laid during early childhood, between birth and the age of seven. In those years, we are like emotional storage, and most of our values come from our parents, family, and social activities or from traumatic experiences we might face. But why do values matter?

Values matter because they define what fulfillment and success mean for each of us. Everyone has a different definition of success and fulfillment. When you know your values, you understand what you need to achieve to attain them. Values give you the clarity to make decisions. Values guide your choices, your heart, and your mind. When you align your actions and feelings with your values, you will find satisfaction and peace.

How do you discover your values? Ask yourself a very simple question: *What is important in my life?* Sometimes, we don't take the time to ask ourselves questions, especially simple ones. We feel the answers are common sense. But sometimes, common sense is not always common practice. The question might be simple, but the impact is enormous. So, ask yourself, *What is important to you in your life?*

Identify the times you felt proud of yourself. When were they? Maybe it's when you spent time with your family. Maybe it's when you supported your daughter. Or maybe it's when you were on stage and presented something that people appreciated. What's important to you? It's not enough just to identify what you're passionate about. Explore why you feel that way. If family is most important to you, why? What are the emotions that family makes you feel? Love? Security? Whatever your answers, write them down.

When do you feel satisfied and fulfilled? Why? Is it when you hear something positive about yourself? When do you feel that? And when do you feel happy? Who are your top three inspirational role models? Mine are the Islamic thinkers of Andalusia, like Ibn Rushd, and I understand why. They were successful scientists, but they also had an identity. Their lives had meaning and are still celebrated today, and those are my top two values: meaning and legacy. Inspirational models are people you like not because of their status but because of their values. So, when you identify one, ask yourself why you like them. What emotion do they make you feel?

And what is your favorite animal? This sounds like an odd question, but the answer reflects your values. I ask many of my clients this question, and often, they'll say the same animal, such as a horse. But when I ask why, their responses differ. Some people say they like the animal because of its speed. Others say elegance, and still others say pride. These answers indicate their values.

Below is a list of common values. Based on your answers, you can choose your top five values. You might have seen that you have a common answer to several questions. That just means that value is very important in your life. From your list of answers, choose five to seven values and then rank them from most important to least important. The most important value is the one that you cannot live without. The order might change in the future, but which do you value the most right now? This exercise will help you build habits and relationships aligned with your values. You will also use those values when you craft your business.

GROWTH

- Self-development
- Curiosity
- Ambition
- Learning
- Creativity
- Open-mindedness
- Determination
- Innovation
- Wisdom
- Exploration

STATUS

- Success
- Recognition
- Achievement
- Prestige
- Influence
- Authority
- Wealth
- Power
- Fame
- Reputation

RELATIONSHIPS

- Empathy
- Trust
- Communication
- Loyalty
- Respect
- Friendship
- Cooperation
- Compassion
- Understanding
- Bonding

RESILIENCE

- Perseverance
- Flexibility
- Courage
- Tenacity
- Patience
- Strength
- Optimism
- Strategic Thinking:
- Adaptability
- Practicality

ETHICS

- Honesty
- Integrity
- Fairness
- Responsibility
- Justice
- Ethical Behavior
- Transparency
- Accountability
- Adherence
- Moral Principles

VISION

- Love
- Knowledge
- Making a Difference
- Peace
- Freedom:
- Enlightenment
- Giving
- Joy
- Purpose
- Clarity

Remember, values often have shadows, so focus on the bright side.

For example, if your top value is *success*, your greatest fear will be failure. If *uniqueness* is your top value, then normality will be your biggest fear. For *honesty*, the fear might be deception, and for *love*, it could be hate. When you focus on achieving your values, you push the shadow aside because your attention is on the thing you really love. Consequently, you will start to fear less when you act according to your values.

Once you've determined your values, you need to check on them daily. Share your values with your friends and partners, and listen to their feedback. It's also important to align your tasks and responsibilities with your values. Ask yourself, *Why am I reading this? What do I love? What am I doing on social media? Why am I working on this project?* If it aligns with your values, continue what you are doing. If not, stop immediately.

Uncover Your Strengths

Your strengths are the second element of VSP. Strength is defined as a particular way of behaving, thinking, believing, or feeling that is authentic and energizing. This definition comes from Cappfinity CEO Alex Linley, one of the leaders in positive psychology for people and companies. In summary, strengths are things you do well, enjoy doing, and use often, and they also energize you.

Strengths can be anything: reading, writing, speaking, compassion, kindness, or adding a new perspective to ideas. Cappfinity and Alex Linley have compiled a list of 60 strengths and their definitions, which you can use to determine your strengths related to thinking, feeling, and behaving.

1. Thinking Strengths

These strengths focus on how individuals process information, solve problems, and approach tasks:

1. **Adaptable** – Being flexible and open to change.

2. **Analytical** – Analyzing information to understand and solve problems.
3. **Creative** – Thinking outside the box to come up with innovative solutions.
4. **Detail-Oriented** – Focusing on the finer points and ensuring accuracy.
5. **Judgment** – Making considered decisions based on available evidence.
6. **Organized** – Structuring tasks and resources efficiently.
7. **Planful** – Planning ahead and anticipating future needs.
8. **Practical** – Focusing on the practical implications of ideas and actions.
9. **Problem Solver** – Effectively identifying and solving problems.
10. **Resilient** – Recovering quickly from setbacks.
11. **Strategic** – Thinking ahead and developing effective strategies.
12. **Visionary** – Seeing the bigger picture and imagining future possibilities.
13. **Inquisitive** – Being curious and eager to learn.
14. **Innovative** – Introducing new ideas or methods.
15. **Reflective** – Thinking deeply about experiences and learning from them.
16. **Logical** – Reasoning and making decisions based on logic.
17. **Objective** – Being unbiased and making judgments based on facts.
18. **Observant** – Noticing details and changes in the environment.
19. **Conceptual** – Understanding complex concepts and how they interrelate.
20. **Methodical** – Working in a systematic and organized way.

2. Feeling Strengths

These strengths relate to how individuals connect emotionally with their work and others:

1. **Authentic** – Being true to oneself and others.
2. **Caring** – Showing concern for others' well-being.
3. **Committed** – Being dedicated and loyal.
4. **Courageous** – Taking risks and standing up for what you believe in.
5. **Empathetic** – Understanding and sharing the feelings of others.
6. **Enthusiastic** – Being energetic and passionate.
7. **Fair-Minded** – Treating everyone fairly and equally.
8. **Humble** – Being modest and respectful.
9. **Integrity** – Acting with honesty and strong moral principles.
10. **Optimistic** – Expecting the best possible outcome.
11. **Patient** – Being calm and understanding.
12. **Persevering** – Persisting in the face of difficulty.
13. **Reliable** – Being dependable and trustworthy.
14. **Resilient** – Maintaining positive emotions despite adversity.
15. **Self-Assured** – Having confidence in your abilities.
16. **Self-Controlled** – Managing emotions and impulses.
17. **Self-Motivated** – Driven to achieve goals.
18. **Trusting** – Believing in others and giving them the benefit of the doubt.
19. **Grateful** – Appreciating what you have.
20. **Respectful** – Valuing others and their contributions.

3. Relating Strengths

These strengths emphasize how individuals interact with and influence others:

1. **Communicative** – Expressing ideas and feelings effectively.
2. **Collaborative** – Working well with others to achieve common goals.
3. **Confident** – Being self-assured and assertive.

4. **Connector** – Bringing people together and creating relationships.
5. **Diplomatic** – Handling situations with tact and sensitivity.
6. **Encouraging** – Supporting and motivating others.
7. **Influential** – Persuading others to your point of view.
8. **Inspiring** – Motivating others to achieve their best.
9. **Leadership** – Guiding and directing a group toward a goal.
10. **Listener** – Being attentive and understanding what others are saying.
11. **Networker** – Building and maintaining relationships.
12. **Persuasive** – Convincing others to support your ideas or actions.
13. **Supportive** – Providing help and encouragement to others.
14. **Team-Oriented** – Prioritizing the group's success over individual goals.
15. **Inclusive** – Ensuring everyone feels valued and included.
16. **Mentoring** – Helping others develop their potential.
17. **Negotiator** – Finding mutually acceptable solutions in conflicts.
18. **Organizational Awareness** – Understanding the dynamics of a group or organization.
19. **Presenter** – Delivering information in a clear and engaging way.
20. **Socially Aware** – Understanding social cues and dynamics.

These strengths can be used in various assessments, coaching sessions, and personal development programs to help individuals understand and maximize their potential in different areas of their lives.

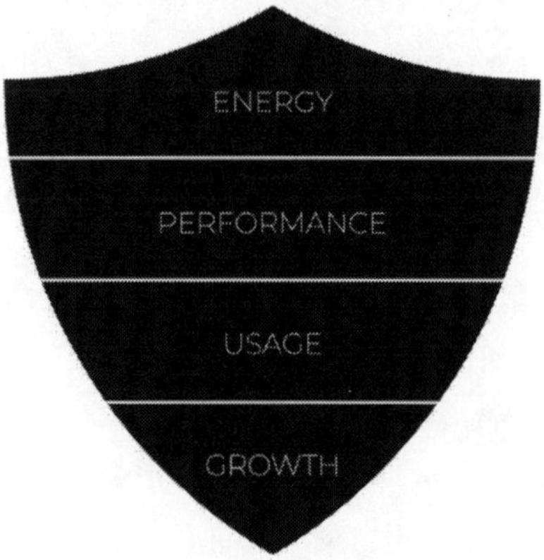

There are four signs that something is a strength.

1. **Energy:** As we mature, we usually force ourselves to develop the areas where we're weak. Our strengths, however, are the things we really like to do and energize us when we do them.
2. **Performance:** One of the most obvious signs that something is a strength is that you are good at it—and you know you are.
3. **Usage:** You like to do this skill or activity, and you do it often.
4. **Growth:** In other words, you develop your skills in this area. Usually, we develop ourselves in areas that we love and that we feel are energizing.

Numerous studies have highlighted the importance of using strengths for people and teams. For example, a Gallup study discovered that people who are using their strengths are six times as likely to be engaged in their jobs, six times as likely to do what they do best every day, and three times as likely to say they have an excellent quality of life. Most importantly, people who use their strengths are more confident, not just in their jobs but in their lives. Teams that use their strengths have 14% to 29% higher profits, 14% to 29% higher employee engagement, and 26% to 72% lower turnover (based on a 2020 Gallup survey). Using your strengths will not only help you excel in what you do, but it will make you happier and more fulfilled.

Positive psychology uses another term called the "flow state," where you feel engaged in what you're doing. Most people don't know how to reach this flow state. Mihaly Csikszentmihalyi, a researcher in positive psychology, wrote a great book about it called *Flow: The Psychology of Optimal Experience.* In the book, he says that people in the flow state are so involved in an activity that nothing else seems to matter. Athletes often call it "being in the zone." You can achieve it by using your strengths.

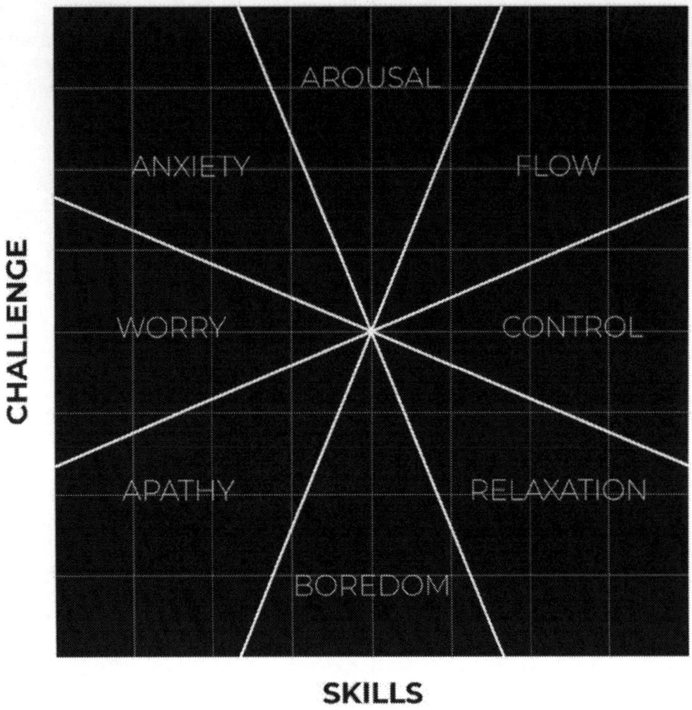

Having very low strengths and no challenges leads to apathy. On the other hand, having high strengths but not enough challenges leads to relaxation. However, having very low skills and very high challenges creates anxiety. For example, if you don't know how to speak in public but have to make an important presentation, your lack of skill combined with the pressure of the situation will make you feel worried and anxious.

The zone we aim for is the one where your strengths match the challenges, or even build on them or encourage you to look for new ones. This zone is called the flow. When you use your strengths to overcome challenges, you will enjoy what you're doing and feel more engaged.

So, how can you identify your strengths? First, ask yourself, "When do I feel fully engaged?" Is it when you are speaking, teaching, or motivating other people? Is it when you feel compassionate about someone or something? Or is it when you participate in a competition? What activities bring positive energy into your life? Communicating with others? Showing courage? Being creative? Making people laugh?

Check the list of 60 strengths and choose the most relevant strengths based on your answers. You can also take the survey on the Strengths Profile website to identify your top strengths and weaknesses.

List of the 60 strengths from StrengthsProfile

- Action
- Curiosity
- Adaptable
- Detail
- Adherence
- Drive
- Adventure
- Emotional Awareness
- Authenticity
- Empathic
- Bounceback
- Enabler
- Catalyst
- Equality
- Centred
- Esteem Builder
- Change Agent
- Explainer
- Compassion
- Feedback
- Competitive
- Gratitude
- Connector
- Growth
- Counterpoint
- Humility
- Courage
- Humor
- Creativity
- Improver

- Incubator
- Prevention
- Innovation
- Pride
- Judgment
- Rapport Builder
- Legacy
- Relationship Deepener
- Listener
- Resilience
- Mission
- Resolver
- Moral Compass
- Self-awareness
- Narrator
- Self-belief
- Optimism
- Service
- Organiser
- Spotlight
- Persistence
- Strategic Awareness
- Personal Responsibility
- Time Optimiser
- Personalization
- Unconditionality
- Persuasion
- Work Ethic
- Planner
- Writer

As we said, strengths are things you are good at, and you know you are good at it. So, what do you do best? What do other people say you are good at? Sometimes, you don't know what you are good at. You have a limiting belief and are missing this affirmation. So, ask people around you, "What do you think I'm good at?" Asking these questions will help you identify your authentic strengths, things you can do, things you would like to do, and things that energize you when you are doing them.

Now that you know your strengths, select five to ten and rank them based on how much energy they give you. What strength gives you the highest energy? Make that number one, and then do the same for numbers two, three, four, and five.

After ranking your strengths, the next step is to understand them. What does each strength mean? What is the definition of that strength, and how does it work? Once you've defined each strength, it's time to share them with your friends, employees, and partners and ask for feedback. Do these strengths make sense? Are they parts of your personality? Do they see those strengths in you as well?

The next step is crucial: You must align your tasks with your strengths. If you find yourself with tasks or projects, focus on leveraging your strengths to tackle them efficiently. By identifying and using your inherent abilities and skills, you can significantly expedite the achievement of your goals and completion of tasks. Because your strength is something you love doing, you enjoy doing, and that energizes you, using it can give you a new perspective on the task at hand. You won't be doing the task just for the sake of doing it; you will enjoy yourself. This is the heart of being a **Human Entrepreneur**.

Finally, it's time to refocus. Sometimes, you need to develop your weaknesses, but before you attempt to do so, think about your strengths. Can you use your strengths to overcome your weaknesses or not? Believe it or not, one of my weaknesses is persistence. I have been leading training sessions almost every week. I also do a live workshop and have coaching sessions every day. When I say persistence is my weakness, some people don't believe me because I'm active on social media, I'm active with my clients, I'm active with my employees, and I'm doing different things simultaneously. It's not about persistence, but it's about using my strengths. It's about growth. It's about a mission. It's about meaning. It's about compassion. I don't focus on persistence. Instead, I use my strengths to overcome my weaknesses and encourage you to do the same.

It's important to realize that you will never turn a weakness into a strength. Why? Because, as we said in the definition, strengths are natural. For example, say you are right-handed. If you decide to develop your ability to use your left hand, it's possible that, with time, you will eventually attain the same adeptness you have with your right. However, using your left hand will never feel as natural to you as using your right hand. This is the difference between developing a weakness and focusing on your strengths.

Now, how can leaders and managers use strengths with their employees and teams? First, don't assume that employees know their strengths. People often take their most powerful talents for granted or are even unaware of them. So, ask your employees what their strengths are, but also try to spot them yourself or identify them using the test at the Strengths Profile website.

Once you've identified your employees' strengths, assign team projects and responsibilities based on them. Incorporate strengths into performance conversations and reviews. Help employees to set goals based on their strengths and align their projects with them. Finally, adopt strength-based teamwork.

We often hear the "teamwork" mantra or slogan. For me, teamwork is when everyone uses their strengths and covers for each other's weaknesses as well. My weakness could be your strength, and my strength could be your weakness. If we really are a team, we will cover for each other. When we align our tasks and projects to maximize our strengths and minimize our weaknesses, that is true teamwork.

What Is Passion?

The third part of the VSP philosophy is passion. What is passion? According to Wikipedia, passion is a feeling of intense enthusiasm toward or compelling desire for someone or something. So, it's a feeling, and we know that emotions change. They are not constant. This means that passion will sometimes fade with time. Barbara Fredrickson—a distinguished professor of psychology, renowned for her research in emotions and positive psychology—highlights passion as a positive emotion in her book *Positivity: Discover the Upward Spiral That Will Change Your Life.*

Yes, passion will give you positive emotions, but at the end of the day, it's a feeling, and feelings can change. That's why I combine values, strengths, and passions. Sometimes, *why* you love is more important than *what* you love.

To discover your passions, ask yourself the following basic questions. Basic questions will sometimes give you the deepest answers you are looking for.

- What are your interests?
- What do you love?
- What were your interests in the past?
- What are the kinds of jobs you could do forever if money and success were guaranteed? Is it fashion? Is it calligraphy? Is it fitness? Is it Zumba? Is it energy healing?
- What activities completely absorb your attention?
- What activities excite you?
- What types of books and courses do you enjoy the most?
- What do you really love?
- What were your interests when you were a child? Maybe you forgot that in this busy world.

Try to answer these questions without any bias, and don't think about entrepreneurship at the moment. Just listen to your heart. Listen to your soul.

Once you've made a list of passions, select five to seven and rank them based on how much energy and enjoyment they give you.

List of Passions:

ART

- Architecture
- Acting
- Voice over
- Singing
- Calligraphy
- Interior Design
- Drawing
- Coloring
- Fashion
- Graphic design
- Photography
- Sculpture
- Collecting Antiques
- Collecting Artwork
- Home Organization
- Magic
- Car Designing
- Media production

SELF HELP

- Happiness
- Hypnosis
- Memory Improvement
- Stress Management
- Time Management
- Writing
- Coaching
- Training
- Communication
- Speaking
- NLP
- Emotional Intelligence

FOOD

- Cooking
- Natural/Organic Foods
- Eating/tasting
- Cake Decorating

HEALTH

- Alternative Medicine
- Weight Loss
- Fitness
- Zumba
- Nutrition Psychology
- Positive Psychology
- Relaxing
- Life style
- Energy healing

BUSINESS

- Economics
- Data Analysis
- Finance
- Investing
- Leadership
- Human Resources
- Marketing/Branding
- Real Estate
- Entrepreneurship
- Business analysis

HISTORY & GEOGRAPHY

- Ancient History
- Geography
- Modern History
- Biographies

CRAFTS & ACCESSORIES

- Flower Arranging
- Jewelry making
- Metal Work
- Painting
- Paper crafts
- Pottery
- Printmaking
- Toy Making
- Wood Working
- Crochet

SCIENCE

- Agricultural
- Archaeology
- Astronomy
- Biology
- Chemistry
- Geology
- Philosophy
- Mathematics

PHYSICS

- Technology
- Engineering

COMPUTER SCIENCE

- Hardware
- Mobile
- Networks
- Programming
- Software
- Web Development
- Electronics

ENTERTAINMENT

- Animals
- Movies

PARENTING

- Family Activities
- Pregnancy & Childbirth
- Special Needs
- Teens

SPORTS

- Ping Pong
- Chess
- Football
- Tennis
- Belly Dancing
- Cave Diving
- Martial arts

RELATIONSHIPS

- Wedding planning
- Relationships
- Dating
- Friendship
- Marriage
- Parenting & Families

PROFESSIONS

- Civil Service
- Education
- Teaching
- Law
- Nursing
- Medical

SPIRITUALITY

- Meditation
- Yoga

OTHERS

- Music
- Games
- Radio
- TV watching
- News/Magazines
- Shopping
- Sleeping

Psychologist Robert J. Sternberg developed the triangle theory of love, which states that there are two main types of love. The first is passionate love. Associated with intense emotions and physical attraction, passionate love typically occurs in the early stages of relationships, and we all know that, right? The second type of love is companion love, characterized by a deeper emotional connection, trust, and long-term commitment, making it a more stable and enduring form of love.

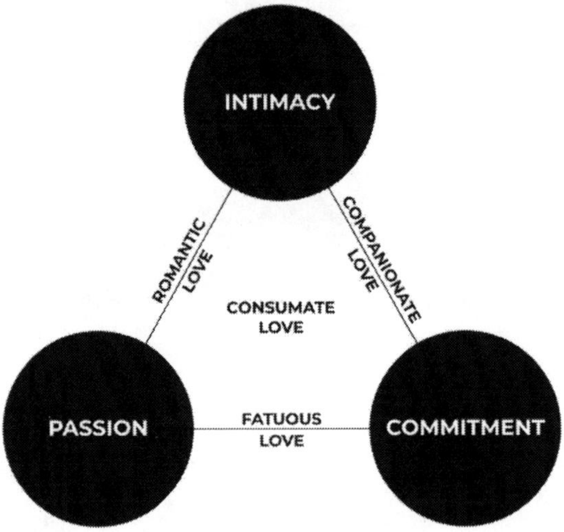

Relationships often transition from passionate love to companion love as they mature over time. Think about it. Lots of people are passionate about certain business ideas. However, what happens for 65% of those people in the first few years, based on data from the U.S. Bureau of Labor Statistics (BLS), is that they lose their momentum. Why? Because they don't know the connection between their values, strengths, and passions. The people who don't give up, those who succeed, don't call what they feel a "passion" anymore. They call it a "companion," like a partner. They've made a long-term commitment, which is exactly what psychologist Robert Sternberg explains in his triangle theory of love. The magic happens when you transition from passionate love to companion love. And you do that by aligning your VSP.

What do you do after determining your passions? First is practice. Practice your top five or seven passions. This is just good for your health and your mental and emotional stability. Then, it's time to test your passions. If you have five, if you have seven, if you have ten, test them. Which of your passions gives you the highest level of energy and the most enjoyment? Once you determine that, you can mark them on your calendar and play privately.

You don't need to have a business behind every passion, just as you don't need a passion behind every business. If you do, perfect, but if you don't, just enjoy doing it. For example, I love ancient history. Can I make a business from ancient history? Yes, but for now, I'm just enjoying reading about it, understanding the philosophies, and becoming empowered by the stories. Some people just enjoy playing a sport, for example. Do they need to create a business around it? The answer is yes for some people, but for others, it's no. They just enjoy doing it.

After identifying and testing your passion, the next step is to find a partner. Sometimes, you will procrastinate, and other times, you'll be overwhelmed with other tasks and issues, so it's essential to find a partner who will push you and share your passion. This will encourage you to keep practicing your passion.

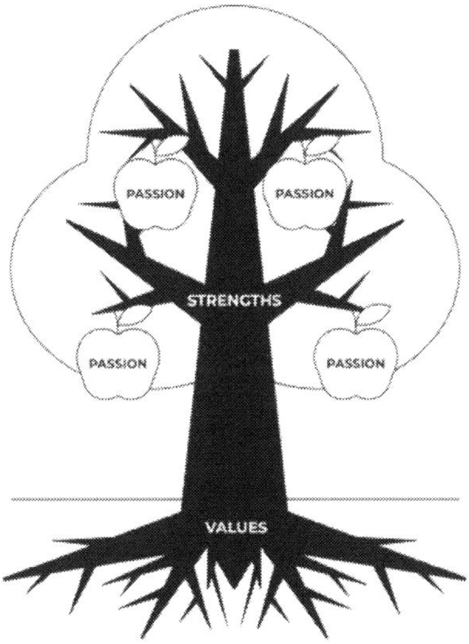

The Tree Metaphor: Aligning Your VSP

Now, let's put it all together. I have adapted the tree metaphor from Dr. Robert Biswas-Diener, a renowned speaker and author on positive psychology. The tree metaphor combines values, strengths, and passions.

I spend much of my time enjoying the outdoors, and I love trees. Entrepreneurs are much like trees, each embarking on a unique journey of growth. Trees stand tall against the wind and reach for the sky against the pull of gravity. To overcome the challenges they face, entrepreneurs, too, must root themselves solidly in the ground and grow against the pull of outside forces. This not only allows them to grow and thrive but also to provide life for others.

The Rooted Values

At the heart of every tree's strength lies its roots, firmly anchored in the soil. For entrepreneurs, these roots represent their values, the guiding principles and beliefs that form their core identity. These values are the bedrock of their journey, providing stability and nourishment. Just as a tree's roots are hidden from view but vital for its growth, your values, which are the foundation of what you build in your entrepreneurial identity, are also hidden. People sometimes don't know about them, but they still give you what you need to grow while staying firmly grounded.

The Soil

The soil surrounding the roots is your family, friends, and beliefs. It's the nurturing environment that provides essential elements for the tree to grow. That's why it's crucial to think about your soil and how you get the supporting elements you need.

The Strong Branches

The branches of the tree are your strengths, providing stability and support for your ideas and passions. They reach for the skies just as you harness your strengths to pursue your dream. The fruit that grows from these branches is what you give to the world: your dreams. People sometimes move from one tree to another because they believe that the fruit growing from their original tree no longer looks appetizing—or even edible—but has withered. Why is that? It's not because of a weakness of their passion or the quality of their ideas. It's because the tree is not functioning.

The fruit withers because it is not receiving nourishment from the soil, roots, and branches. There is no harmony between your values, strengths, and passions. That's why your dreams lose their momentum with time. However, when you have this connection, your ideas will stay alive.

When clients tell me, "I need to find my passion," or "I need to find a career," I look at their VSP card. I call it a VSP card because it's like an identity card. My hope is that they can attach their values, strengths, and passions to their identity.

AHMED

Values	Strengths	Passions
Fairness	Adventure	Leadership
Equality	Connector	Art-drawing
freedom	Gratitude	Social interaction
Support	Spotlight	
Cooperation	Compassion	
Knowledge	Counterpoint	
Openness	Mission	
Exploration	Growth	
Adventure	Rapport builder	

SALMA

Values	Strengths	Passions
Sense of meaning	Improver	Leadership
Faith	Curiosity	Parenting
Love	Growth	Entrepreneurship
Freedom	Creativity	Scuba diving
Wisdom	Persuasion - Spotlight	Sky diving
Peace	Courage	Meditation
Success	Strategic awareness	
Achievement	Competitive	

Sometimes, when two people have the same business idea, passion, or career, they compete against each other. However, there is usually no need for this. For example, I have a client named Ahmed. His top three values are *Fairness, Equality,* and *Freedom.* His top three strengths are *Adventure, Connector,* and *Gratitude.* His top passion is *Leadership.*

Let's compare that with Sarah, whose top three values are a *Sense of meaning, Faith,* and *Love.* Her top three strengths are *Improvement, Curiosity,* and *Growth.* Her top passion is also *Leadership.* But the flavor of leadership for Sarah is different than it is for Ahmed. If Ahmed were to compare his leadership style to Sarah's, there would be a mismatch. For Sarah, leadership comes from *Meaning, Faith, Love, Improvement, Curiosity,* and *Growth.* But for Ahmed, leadership comes from *Sternness, Equality, Freedom, Adventure, Connection,* and *Gratitude.* From this, we can see that when you know your tree and the connection between your values, strengths, and passions, you don't compete; you just live and give.

Discover Your Career Anchors

Noted social psychologist and MIT Sloan professor Dr. Edgar Schein's theory of the career anchor is a profound concept concerning people's motivations and career choices. Schein's research revealed that people have distinct career anchors, fundamental patterns, or dimensions in their work. These anchors reflect their values, needs, strengths, and passions, providing a foundation for career satisfaction and fulfillment.

There are eight types of career anchors.

1. **Technical-functional:** This type of person likes being good at something and will work to become a guru or expert.
2. **Managerial competence:** These people want to be managers. They like problem-solving and dealing with other people.
3. **Entrepreneurial creativity:** These people like to invent things, be creative, and, most of all, run their own businesses.
4. **Service or dedication to a cause:** Service-oriented people are driven more by how they can help others than by their strengths
5. **Autonomy and independence:** These people have a primary need to work under their own rules. They avoid standards and prefer to work alone.

6. **Pure challenge:** People driven by challenges seek constant stimulation and difficult problems they can tackle. Such people will change jobs when the current one gets boring, and their careers can be varied.
7. **Lifestyle:** Those who are focused on lifestyle look at their whole pattern of living and are more likely to integrate work and life than others.
8. **Security & Stability:** These people seek stability and continuity as a primary factor in their lives. They avoid risk and are generally "lifers" in their job.

Think about your values, strengths, and passions. What is your primary career anchor? Recall a job that you really liked. Why did you like it? Now think about a job that you really hated. Why did you hate it? Was it because you couldn't find your primary career anchor there? And if you liked a particular job, was it because your career anchor was present there?

After reflecting on your answers to these questions, select at least one primary and one secondary career anchor and see if you can align them with your values, strengths, and passions.

Do you see a link? Because you will.

Selecting a Winning Business Idea

Generating a business idea can be exciting and doubtful. However, by harnessing the power of three core concepts—problem-solving, tapping into your values, strengths, and passions, and staying attuned to current business trends—you can unlock the door to the world of entrepreneurial opportunities.

1. **Solving a problem:** Every successful business is, at its core, a solution to a problem. Think about it. From the smartphone you hold in your hand to the app that helps you find your home, innovations address specific issues or needs. Consider the problem that resonates with you most. What challenges do people face in their daily lives? What

pain points can you alleviate? Identifying problems and striving for solutions is an excellent starting point for generating business ideas. Start with a problem.

2. **Check your VSP:** Your values, strengths, and passions are your inner compass guiding you toward ideas that align with your authentic self. Values represent what matters most to you. Strengths showcase your abilities, and passions reveal the activities that ignite your enthusiasm. By diving into your VSP, you can highlight potential ideas. For example, if you like public speaking, you can talk about public speaking. If you are creative, you can make things like homemade candles or accessories. Use your VSP as a guiding force for your brainstorming.
3. **Shop around:** The business world is constantly changing, with trends and innovations shaping industries daily. Keeping a watchful eye on these trends can inspire fresh ideas and provide insights into emerging markets. Follow industry publications, attend relevant conferences, and engage in conversation with your field.

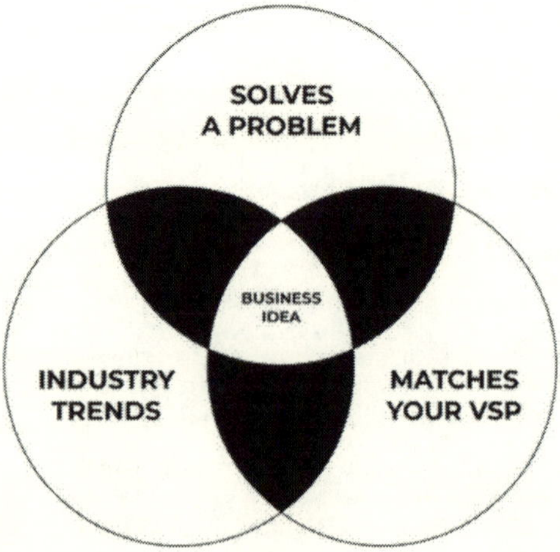

The best business idea solves a problem, matches your VSP, and aligns with industry trends. To come up with your own great idea, link these three concepts. When you do, you will find the sweet spot: an idea that can build a good business.

People approach me sometimes with the same business idea. One of them, let's call her Mariam, had a burning passion for helping others build meaningful connections and was committed to her vision. She believed in herself and her abilities, even when faced with challenges. Another client, let's call him John, had the same idea but had limiting beliefs and lacked the commitment to see it through. His journey ended quickly. Mariam managed to start her business while John struggled. This story illustrates a fundamental truth: A strong business idea is as much about the entrepreneur as it is about the concept. Your mindset, commitment, and belief in your idea can make all the difference.

Now, if you're a brainstormer and come up with plenty of ideas, how do you choose one? When it comes to selecting the right business idea, several factors come into play. Here are the key criteria to consider.

1. **Passion:** Choose something you are genuinely passionate about. Your enthusiasm will fuel your dedication and resilience during the entrepreneurial journey.
2. **Importance:** Assess the idea's significance in addressing a real problem or need. Businesses that solve real problems tend to thrive.
3. **Profitability:** Ensure that your idea has the potential to generate revenue and be financially sustainable. It should align with your financial goals.
4. **Scalability:** Consider whether your idea can grow over time and whether there is room for expansion. Scalable businesses have great potential for long-term success. You need to think about how to use technology in your idea because, with technology, you can easily scale your business.
5. **Lifestyle:** Think about the lifestyle you desire. Your business idea should align with your personal and professional goals.

Aligning your idea with your VSP allows you the flexibility and freedom you seek, and you can actually rate that. Rate each of your business ideas from zero to ten in terms of passion, importance, profitability, scalability, and lifestyle.

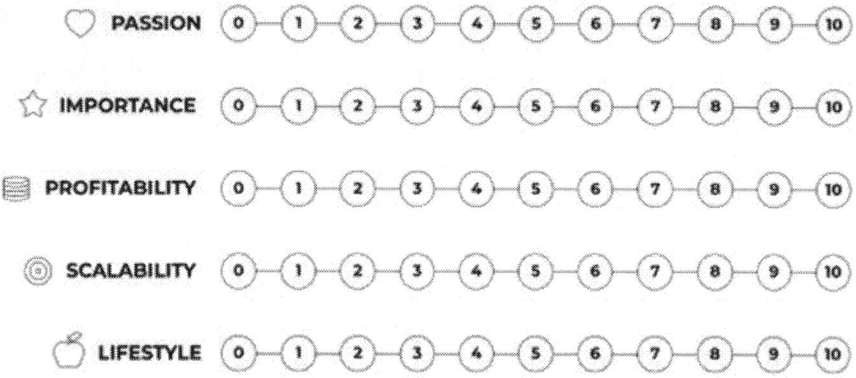

Find the idea with the highest score and use it because there is no such thing as a good or bad business idea. You can make it work if you have the right mindset and the basic foundation for the idea to succeed, as highlighted in these five important factors.

Conclusion

In this chapter, we explored the first stage, **Uncover**. This stage focuses on recognizing our core values, strengths, and passions, which lays a strong foundation for achieving satisfaction and fulfillment by transforming our career paths or selecting a business idea for our start-up. Sometimes, the challenge we face is ensuring that our career and business align with our true identity, which helps us overcome any obstacle.

In Chapter 2, we enter the next stage, **Explore**, where we will learn the eight elements we can use to determine whether our chosen business idea is fit enough to proceed with.

Exercise:

List your top seven values, strengths, and passions in sequence on the Values, Strengths, and Passions (VSP) card. Additionally, clearly write your primary and secondary career anchors to gain deeper insight into your professional aspirations and personal growth trajectory.

CHAPTER 2

Explore: Widen Your Vision

"Wonder is the beginning of wisdom."
– Socrates

Cultivating an Exploration Mindset

In this chapter, we will take a step toward cultivating your business idea by exploring what you need to look at to transform your idea into one you can build your business around. Entrepreneurs are not only business experts; they are explorers. They search for opportunities and make smart choices. To succeed on this journey, you will need to become an explorer, too.

Great explorers and successful entrepreneurs have three important traits: curiosity, courage, and conviction.

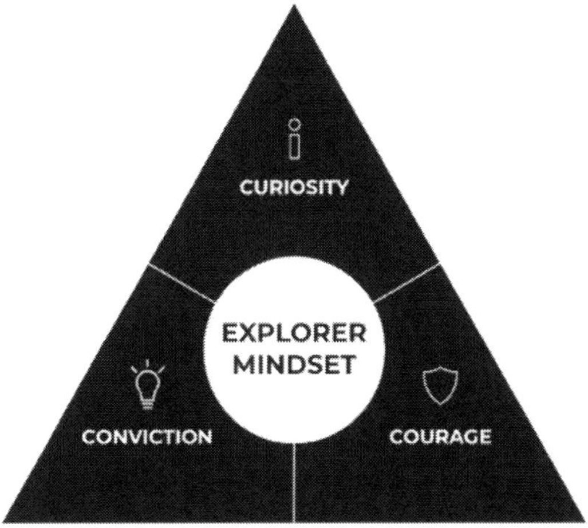

1. **Curiosity:** Explorers desire to learn, discover, and ask questions. They are always wondering why things are the way they are. They are excited about what they don't know and want to fill the gaps in their knowledge. Sometimes, they must face their limiting beliefs and fears, but when they do, they're eager to find answers.
2. **Courage:** Explorers are brave. They face challenges and venture into the unknown. They are not afraid to take risks, even when things seem scary or uncertain. This is not because they have no fear. They feel fear just like everyone else, but they push forward anyway. *Fear the Fear and Do It Anyway* by Susan Jeffers is a great book if you'd like to dig deeper into the concept.
3. **Conviction:** This is about believing in yourself and your ideas. Conviction is the firm belief that you are on the right path, even when others doubt you. It's like having a strong inner compass that guides you. Conviction comes from using your VSP as your guiding force.

The story of Christopher Columbus is a perfect example of how these traits can lead to incredible discoveries. Columbus lived in a time when people believed the world was flat and nobody knew what lay beyond the vast oceans. But he was curious. He wanted to find a new route to Asia by sailing west. Columbus was incredibly courageous, too. He convinced others to join him on his journey across the Atlantic Ocean, even though they feared falling off the edge of the world. Columbus believed in his idea with unwavering conviction. Some researchers say that he also studied the old maps of the Andalusian scientists and sailors, gathering as much knowledge as possible to prepare himself for the unknown.

And guess what happened? Columbus sailed into uncharted waters and discovered a whole new land. His curiosity, courage, conviction, and the knowledge he gained from the journey changed the course of history.

The Eight Elements of Exploration

Exploration is an essential aspect of many fields, including entrepreneurship and the oil and gas industry. In the world of entrepreneurship, exploration is like a compass that guides you through unknown and uncharted territories. It is a journey of discovery, where you must navigate through obstacles and find innovative solutions to problems that arise.

Exploration is the first step in drilling for resources in the oil and gas industry. Before drilling, the earth must be examined to make informed and cost-effective decisions. The examination involves analyzing the earth's depth, composition, and condition to determine the best approach to extracting valuable resources. This process helps ensure that the drilling operation is successful and profitable.

Exploration is crucial to the success of any venture and is a vital part of risk management. It helps entrepreneurs identify potential opportunities and threats and make informed decisions about resource allocation and investment. By exploring new territories, entrepreneurs can discover untapped markets and create innovative products and services that meet the needs of consumers.

Exploration is not just about discovering new territories but also about pushing the boundaries of what is possible. It requires creativity, innovation, and a willingness to take risks. Successful entrepreneurs are fearless in stepping outside their comfort zones and exploring new ideas, even if they face failure along the way.

The exploration phase is a vital component of the **IdentityBrand Cycle**, ensuring that your business is rooted in knowledge, strategy, and purpose.

Now, as an entrepreneur, you are stepping into an unknown land, the market of your chosen industry. To prepare for your journey, consider these eight key elements of exploration. They are the fundamental elements you need when you explore, along with the three traits already mentioned: curiosity, courage, and conviction.

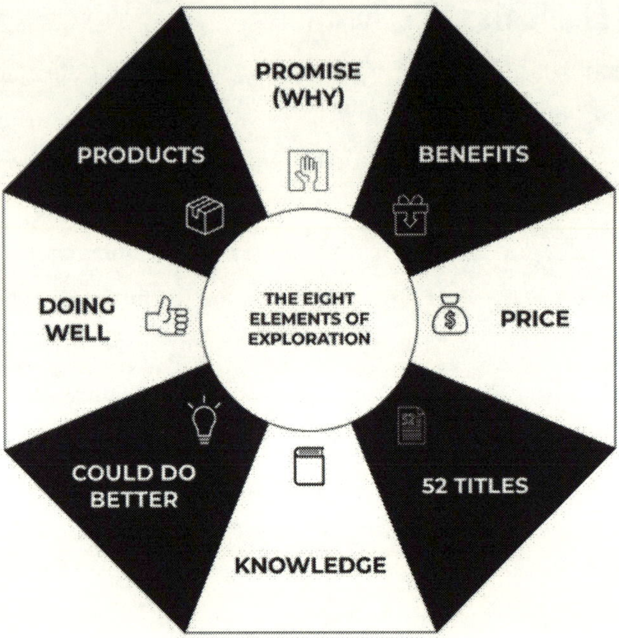

1. **Check the products in the market.** Examine what products are already available in your industry. This could include online courses, consultations, toolkits, retreats, planners, and more. These exciting offers can inspire ideas for your next step. Write them down, as you will need them for the next few steps.

____

____

____

____

____

____

____

2. **Study the promises made by successful competitors.** These promises can often be found on their websites or in their social media campaigns. They provide insight into what your audience values and what they are willing to pay for. The homepage of Squarespace, a prominent web design company, is a prime example:

   CREATE YOUR WEBSITE

   The leader in website design – Stand out online with a professional website, online store, or portfolio. With Squarespace, you can turn any idea into a reality.

   Another example is the content found on the Shopify homepage:

   Making Commerce Better for Everyone

   Shopify is supporting the next generation of entrepreneurs, the world's biggest brands, and everyone in between

3. **Explore the benefits offered to customers.** Companies' benefits are displayed on their websites, social media pages, and platforms and in their marketing materials. Here's an example of benefits offered by a business coach or mentor:

   Learn everything you need to start your own business.

   Map what makes you unique and learn how to use it in business and life.

4. **Determine the price ranges in the market.** Note the price ranges of products and services in your industry. Understanding the price landscape will guide your pricing strategy once you have designed your product or products.

5. **Observe the aspects in which successful individuals or companies excel.** Learn from the achievements of others to inform your approach. Write down what you like. Do you like their website? Do you like their tone of voice? Do you like their copywriting? Do you like a specific technology that they are using? Just write it down.

6. **Identify areas that can be improved**. You have highlighted things that you like, but you should also highlight areas where existing products or services can be improved. You can get that information from customer feedback, reviews, and market trends.

7. **Boost your knowledge.** To make continuous learning a priority, consider enrolling in courses relevant to your chosen industry. Additionally, delve into industry-related books, attend webinars for updates, and immerse yourself in learning the language specific to your field. By taking these proactive steps, you can stay abreast of the latest trends and developments while expanding your expertise.

8. **Collect data from various sources.** Collecting things like videos, podcasts, articles, and books within your industry can significantly benefit your content strategy. This practice has been instrumental in my growth, prompting me to recommend it to my clients as well. By curating this wealth of information, you not only stay abreast of trends but also fuel your creativity for future social media posts and content creation. This proactive approach ensures you never face a blank page, as you always have a repository of ideas to draw from, including insights and inspirations from others that can be incorporated into your own products or projects.

I recommended manually collecting data before using AI tools. While AI tools may seem straightforward, manually gathering data will help shape your mindset. By observing, listening, and gathering data firsthand, you can gain a deeper understanding of your industry. It's not just about understanding your industry; it's about cultivating the right mindset. How can you develop a mindset without observing and taking risks? Once you've gathered your data, AI can help uncover trends, refine your insights, and generate valuable information.

As your company progresses with an exploratory mindset, embrace curiosity, courage, and unwavering conviction. These traits will be your guiding stars on this entrepreneurial journey; through them, you will harness the power of the exploratory mindset.

Talk to People

To better explore your idea, consider connecting with potential customers and industry peers for feedback. Engage with at least three people in your industry—this could be during mentorship, in casual conversation, or even through email.

Once you've gathered the positives and negatives of the industry, identify common trends. Compare these insights with your initial beliefs about the business concept. Can you handle any potential drawbacks, and do the positives still ignite your excitement as they did initially? Seek feedback from friends, family members, and colleagues. Their perspectives can help refine your ideas. For instance, in his book *Will It Fly?* Pat Flynn describes how he initially planned to create a website for food truck owners. However, after receiving feedback indicating a lack of credibility due to his not owning a food truck, he adapted his concept to become a community curator for food truck owners.

Allow Yourself to Get Lost

Embrace the thrilling adventure of exploration on your entrepreneurial journey. During a business trip to Aberdeen, Scotland, I found myself deviating from my usual detailed travel plans. Rather than meticulously scheduling every sight to see, I unexpectedly stumbled upon the magnificent Dunnottar medieval fortress by the North Sea. Despite not being part of my initial itinerary, this unplanned discovery turned into an unforgettable experience.

The castle, nestled along the beautiful coastline, provided a picturesque backdrop complemented by perfect weather. I spent the entire afternoon at this enchanting location, forgoing other planned visits for the day. It was a serendipitous encounter that added a touch of magic to my trip, reminding me of the joy found in spontaneity and exploration.

The lesson here is don't be afraid to get a little lost on your journey. Just as my detour led to an unexpected scene, your willingness to explore the unknown can lead to great discoveries. Embrace uncertainty. It often holds the keys to your success.

With curiosity, courage, and conviction as your guides, your journey will be filled with exciting exploration and valuable insights. As we continue in this book, we will dive deeper into the heart of entrepreneurship, uncovering the secrets of the **IdentityBrand Cycle**.

As we conclude Chapter 2, we've explored the essential mindset for expanding your entrepreneurial horizons. Embracing curiosity and courage enables you to uncover new opportunities that resonate with your values and ambitions. This journey of discovery not only enhances your business but also fosters personal growth. With a broader perspective, you're now prepared to move forward and define the core of your business identity in the next chapter. Let's continue to explore and refine your vision, building a foundation for lasting success.

Exercise:

Remember a situation where you found yourself lost and had to detour from your original plan. Reflect on the experience and consider what valuable lessons you learned from that unexpected turn. Take some time to jot down the top three lessons you learned from navigating that detour.

CHAPTER 3

Define: The Birth of Your Business

"Knowledge is not complete until it is passed on."
– Ibn Rushd (Averroes), Andalusian polymath

Entrepreneurship is a journey that takes you through various phases, each with unique challenges and opportunities. That's why my favorite statement is, "Welcome challenges." They're coming, so you need to welcome them and learn from them.

In the previous chapter, we embarked on the exploration phase, equipping ourselves with the curious and open-minded mindset of an explorer. Now, we step into the defining phase, where the treasures of your entrepreneurial dreams begin to take shape. In this phase, you will reflect on what you learned during the exploration phase and establish the foundation of your business.

Once again, you can compare this process to the oil and gas industry. After exploring a large area, it's time to select a location to start drilling. It's a milestone because you choose a specific part of a wide area to test your model. This focused area in oil and gas is called a lead. In this chapter, we will explore how to define the sweet spot you will focus on to generate your business idea.

Defining Your Ideal Partner/Customer

This is a critical aspect of your business, trip, or journey. It helps you navigate the vast ocean of possibilities by providing clarity about who you would like to serve. This clarity is essential because it directs your effort toward the people who matter most to your business and you. When you understand your ideal customer, you can communicate with them in a way that resonates. You will grasp their needs, preferences, and pain points, allowing you to tailor your message for maximum impact and legacy.

Now that we have shown the significance of knowing your ideal customer, let's explore how to define them effectively.

When defining your customer, consider these three key factors.

1. **Problem-solving:** First, you must be confident in your ability to solve your customers' problems. Your business should address their pain points or fulfill their needs. So, you need to select customers whose problems you can solve.

2. **Excitement:** Consider whether you genuinely feel excited about working with your customers, as you will spend a significant amount of time interacting with them. If you lack enthusiasm for working with your current clientele, select a type of customer that energizes you. Building a successful business requires not only dedication to your work but also a genuine enthusiasm for the people you serve.
3. **Financial compatibility:** Assess whether your customers can pay for your products or services or not. While you may have a strong desire to help or serve, your business must also remain financially viable.

It's important to learn everything about your ideal customer. Many business books discuss two factors: demographics and psychographics. The first, demographics, refers to factual information about your customer. It includes characteristics such as age, gender, location, income, education, and occupation, the basics that help categorize your customers.

Psychographics, on the other hand, dives deeper into the psychological aspects of your ideal customer, encompassing their interests, values, lifestyle behaviors, and preferences. Psychographics provide valuable insight into what makes your customers tick and why they make certain choices.

However, what you must truly master is understanding your customers' pain points or problem statements, as they say. By actively listening and collecting information, you can gain valuable insights into your customers' needs and identify any barriers or gaps preventing them from fulfilling those needs, such as limiting beliefs related to money, family, or communication. When you identify those gaps, it's an opportunity to solve them, meaning it's also an opportunity to build a thriving business.

Having a clear image of your ideal customer should guide your communication with them. Successful companies like Dollar Shave Club, Warby Parker, and Beyond Meat have mastered this art. They understand their customers' pains, needs, and desires, allowing them to tailor their offerings effectively.

Dollar Shave Club disrupted the razor industry by understanding the pain points of its target audience: men who were tired of paying high prices for razors. They offered a subscription model for high-quality razors at a reasonable price. Their marketing was witty and relatable, resonating with their audience's desire for value and needs. By solving the problem of overpriced razors and delivering a delightful customer experience, Dollar Shave Club gained a massive following and was eventually acquired by Unilever for $1 billion.

Warby Parker recognized the frustration customers felt when buying eyeglasses (and I'm one of them) due to high costs and limited options. They aim to provide affordable, stylish eyewear while also addressing social concerns by offering a home try-on, cutting out the middlemen, and donating a pair of glasses for every pair sold. They won over the customer base looking for affordability and a sense of social responsibility.

Beyond Meat tapped into the growing demand for plant-based alternatives to meat products. They understood that many customers were concerned about the environmental impact of traditional meat production and wanted something different. Beyond Meat created plant-based burgers and sausages that tasted remarkably very close to real meat. I tried their products with my wife, but she figured it out easily. By aligning with the values of health-conscious and environmentally aware consumers, Beyond Meat became a pioneer in the plant-based food industry. You might not like that, but they know their customers.

These examples showcase how understanding your ideal customer's pain points, needs, and values can lead to innovative solutions and successful businesses. Each of these companies not only identified these factors but also communicated effectively with their target audience, building strong brand connection, identity, and reality.

In conclusion, your customers are more than just points or numbers in your Customer Relationship Management (CRM) software or systems. They are your living partners on this entrepreneurial journey. By genuinely caring about them and understanding their needs, you will not only receive emotional rewards, but your business will also thrive. So, don't collect data for the sake of a project or to reach a target market. Collect data because you care. Collect data because you love helping people. Collect data because you want to give. This shift in perspective will transform how you can help and continue to grow in your entrepreneurial journey.

Exercise:

Write down the top seven pain points, needs, and gaps that your ideal customer faces. Understanding these aspects can help you better tailor your products or services to address their specific challenges and requirements, ultimately leading to a more successful and customer-centric approach.

Defining Your Unique Selling Points

In today's crowded marketplace, simply offering a good product or service isn't enough. You need something that makes you stand out, captures attention, and compels customers to choose you over your competitors. That's why Unique Selling Points (USPs) are very important.

Why Define Your USP?

Your USP isn't about manipulating people. It's about clarity and helping people find you and know what the ultimate benefits are if they decide to work with you.

1. **It focuses your message.** Knowing your unique value helps you craft marketing that speaks directly to the right people and avoids unnecessary noise.
2. **It helps you connect with customers.** Your USP shows your customers that you understand their needs and offer something different, building trust and a genuine connection.
3. **It helps you make confident decisions.** Your core value guides your product development, marketing, and overall direction.

How Do You Define Your USP?

Discovering powerful USPs is key. It starts by deeply understanding customer needs. Use surveys and interviews to identify their frustrations. Then, analyze competitors' characteristics—such as price and innovation—using a scale from zero to ten. Doing this reveals opportunities where you can excel, allowing you to craft a USP focused on marketing and sales that will attract customers who truly resonate with your offering.

What Are the Characteristics of Effective USPs?

1. **Customer-driven:** USPs should be consumer-focused, addressing the customers' specific needs and desires.

2. **Valuable:** They must provide real value to customers, solving their problems or fulfilling their desires.
3. **Unique:** Your USP should distinguish you from competitors, showing what sets you apart or what you choose to set you apart.

While in Las Vegas for a conference, I saw a billboard for *Cirque du Soleil* and decided to watch one of their events. The performance was completely different from the old classic circus. Imagine entering a circus tent, expecting the usual acts of clowns, animals, and acrobats. Then you step into the world of *Cirque du Soleil,* and everything changes. What makes *Cirque du Soleil* stand out? It's a unique entertainment experience. *Cirque du Soleil's* USP lies in its ability to transform a traditional circus into an immersive, artistic, and emotional experience. Instead of relying on animals or typical circus acts, it combines breathtaking acrobats, stunning visuals, and compelling storytelling, which we will discuss in the next chapter.

Their productions are not merely shows. They are journeys into the extraordinary, appealing to a diverse audience seeking more than just traditional entertainment.

Craft Your USPs

Now that you understand the significance of USPs, it's time to craft your own by aligning your unique qualities with your target audience. In our exploration of unique selling points, we have uncovered the importance of setting your business apart from competitors. But USPs are not just catchy slogans or features. They are powerful stories waiting to be told.

The essence of your USPs can be shown through authentic storytelling. Stories have an incredible ability to resonate with your audience on a deeper level, evoking emotions and connections. In the world of marketing and sales, it's not just about promoting your products or services; it's about inviting people into your story. When you embrace the storytelling potential for your USPs, you not only stand out but you create lasting connections with your audience.

Exercise:

List your top three unique selling points for your brand or core products.

"A brand for a company is like a reputation for a person.
You earn reputation by trying to do hard things well."
–Jeff Bezos

Define Your Brand Values

Imagine your brand values as a compass that guides both you and your customers on a journey. They play a vital role in shaping your business, especially its identity. To create a brand that truly resonates with your audience, you must define these values authentically. But why do brand values matter so much? They matter because they serve as the emotional bridge between your business and your customers. Authentic brand values resonate with your customers, creating a sense of alignment and trust. When your values align with theirs, a sale is more than a transaction. It's a partnership built on shared beliefs.

Take the story of Paul O'Neill, the former CEO of Alcoa. When O'Neill focused solely on safety as the company's core value, it transformed Alcoa's culture and profitability from the inside out. By conducting Key Performance Indicators (KPIs), such as assessments, standard operating procedures, and evaluations around safety, Alcoa not only improved workplace conditions but also saw a remarkable increase in profits. This example illustrates the transformative power of emphasizing a single core value. Your value should align with your unique selling points and customer needs, creating a harmonious ecosystem.

When you strike that balance between your values, your unique selling points, and your customers' needs, you've hit the sweet spot. Your brand values will not only guide your decisions but also inspire you and your customers. They are the heart of your business. Just as your personal values are your guiding force, your brand values are the guiding force and the roots of your business.

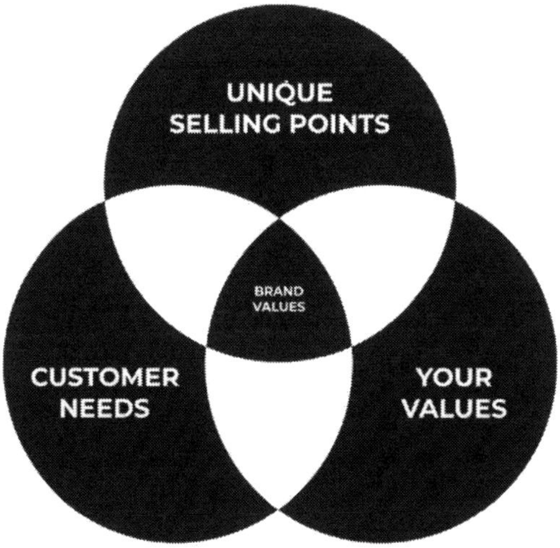

Conclusion

As you craft your brand values, remember this: Authenticity is non-negotiable, who you are genuinely as a business leader and a human. Stay focused on trends and the number of followers you have. Follow your values, craft your brand values, deliver them with authenticity, and win for yourself and your business.

Exercise:

Please list your top five brand values.

CHAPTER 4

Design: Structure Your Message

"Your vision will become clear only when you look into your heart. Who looks outside, dreams; who looks inside, awakes."
– Carl Jung

Welcome to the design phase, the fourth stage in the **IdentityBrand Cycle**. We are here to craft and pick the perfect tools and strategies to bring your brand and business to life. Imagine we are in the oil industry, ready to drill. We have already found where the oil or gas might be in the subsurface, or what is called a potential lead, and where we need to drill. Now, it's about choosing the right tools and people for the job based on what we know about the subsurface.

In this phase, we take all our exploration insights about your product, brand, competitors, and market research and decide on the best tools and approaches to make your vision ready for reality. It's like preparing for a successful drill, ensuring we have everything we need to hit the oil and make it flow. Here is where your brand starts to take tangible form, crafted with precision for the market.

In this chapter, you will learn how to craft your brand and products, just like selecting the proper rig and tools before you drill. We will start by mapping out your one-page product canvas, a tool that helps you visualize the bridge from customer problems to your brand's or product's promises. Next, we'll dive into the art of storytelling with your personal journey.

Highlighting the Design Stage

You will discover how to weave your experience, challenges, and triumphs into a narrative that resonates with your ideal customer, building trust and connection with them. We will also guide you through designing your brand message, ensuring it's clear, compiling, and consistent across all your communications. This is your blueprint for how you talk about your brand, what you stand for, and why customers should listen and care.

Understanding why customers buy is crucial, so we will explore the motivations behind their decisions. This knowledge will help you tailor your offers to meet their needs more effectively and increase the likelihood of success and fulfillment.

Finally, we will discuss the power of surrounding yourself with the right people, from mentors to peers who inspire and support you. We will cover the types of relationships that can help you grow personally and professionally. By the end of this chapter, you will have a solid foundation for designing a brand that not only stands out but also deeply connects with your customers and yourself, setting the stage for success in your business and fulfillment in your heart.

Crafting Your One-Page Product Canvas

Let's dive into the first tool in our kit: the one-page product canvas. This is where you will take all those big ideas floating around and pin them down onto one manageable, actionable page. It is like sketching the blueprint for your dream house. Expect this blueprint to be for your customer's journey from problem to promise.

Start by listing the top three problems your customers face. These are the reasons they are looking for a product or service in the first place. The second step is to end with a promise. Think about the three big promises your product or service makes. These are the reasons your customers will choose yours over any other. The third part is to map the journey. Now that your problems and promises are set, it's time to map out the journey from pain to pleasure for your customer. Think of it as charting a course through uncharted water, guiding your customers to the treasure of your solution.

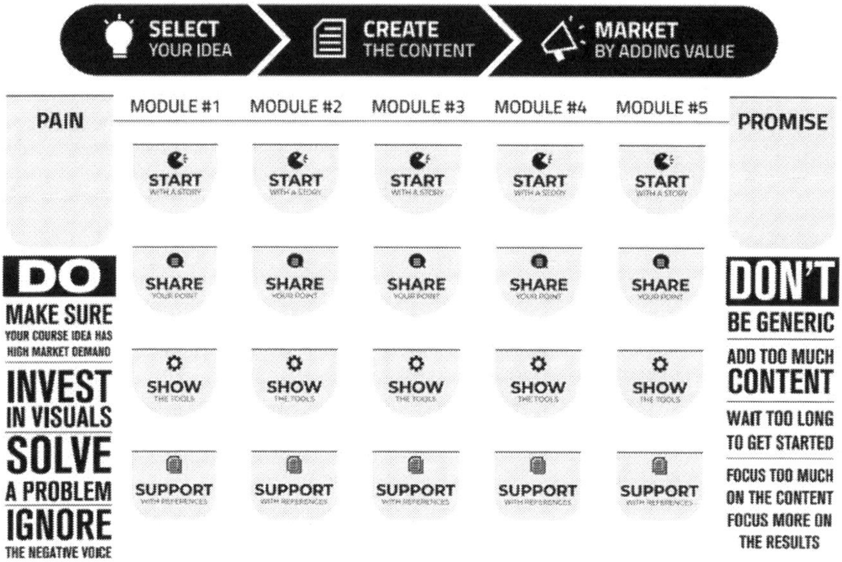

Map everything as much as you can. Build your philosophy and blend all your knowledge in as well. For each step of the journey, give each milestone a name that captures its essence. This is about making the journey memorable and easy to follow. For each step of the journey, you need tools and techniques. List the specific tools or methods you will employ to tackle this leg of the journey. These are your secret weapons to making the promise a reality. Next, pinpoint the essential ideas or principles that need to be shared. This stage is about enlightening your customers and making sure they are with you every step of the way. For each step of the journey, add stories and facts. Weave in narratives that highlight the steps' importance or the value of moving forward. This is about connecting emotionally and logically with your audience.

Your one-page product canvas is more than a document. It's a strategic map of your products or services that lays out how you will guide your customers from their current frustrations to the solution you offer. It's a powerful tool to clearly communicate your value proposition, whether on social media, through marketing materials, in face-to-face conversations, or with your team.

Just like that, you have created a concise, impactful, one-page product canvas that not only outlines your plan but also tells a compelling story of transformation. This is what we are looking for—not just knowledge but blending your expertise with your philosophy so you can help people transform from one state to another. This canvas is your beacon in the marketplace, shining light on your brand and drawing customers to your solutions.

Crafting Your Personal Story

Let's shift gears and focus on one of the most powerful tools in your branding arsenal: your personal story. I've seen thousands of entrepreneurs and businesses all over the world, and I can't stress enough the value of well-crafted personal stories, especially for knowledge-based entrepreneurs, where your knowledge is part of who you are. People don't just buy your knowledge; they buy your attitude and your story. Your journey, with all its ups and downs, turnarounds, and challenges, isn't just a biography. It can guide your customers to trust and connect with your brand on a deeper level.

The Essence of Authenticity

In the digital age, authenticity isn't just a word. It's the queen of connection. Your personal story is a product of your experience, challenges, and triumphs. It's what sets you apart in the world of competition. By sharing your journey, you are not just telling your story; you are extending an invitation into your world, showing your customers the heart behind the brand. A great example is prolific American author Joseph Campbell's "Hero's Journey." In his most famous work, *The Hero with a Thousand Faces*, he introduces the concept of the "Hero's Journey," a universal motif of adventure and transformation that runs through virtually all of the world's mythic traditions. He believed that these recurring patterns and themes are reflective of universal human experiences, often used in storytelling and personal development. His ideas have been widely influential in storytelling and filmmaking. But it isn't just for epic tales and blockbuster movies. It's a framework that can be used to structure your personal story and will help you to become a master storyteller.

This timeless structure starts with a desire, leads through various challenges, introduces guides and mentors, hits a climax of crisis, and concludes with a triumphant return.

1. **The Desire:** Begin by sharing what drove you to start your entrepreneurial journey. Was it a personal challenge, a gap in the market, or a desire for change?
2. **The Problem:** Highlight the obstacles you faced early on. These struggles set the stage for your transformation and make your story relatable.
3. **Meeting the Guide:** Introducing the mentors, books, or experiences that shaped your path. This shows that growth often comes from learning and collaboration.
4. **The Maze and the Crisis:** Share the moments of doubt and challenges that tested your resilience. This will build tension and engagement in your narrative.
5. **The Victory:** Celebrate the breakthroughs and successes. This isn't just about flaunting achievements; it's about showing the possibility of overcoming challenges. You will probably face both external and internal challenges. External challenges could be things like deciding to quit or start your own business, while internal challenges are feelings like fear and doubt. Overcoming internal challenges helps you overcome external ones, too.
6. **The Return:** Eventually, your journey will come full circle, with you now in a position to guide others. This positions you as a trusted authority in your field.

Make Your Story Relevant

The key to a powerful personal story is relevance. Choose aspects of your journey that mirror the challenges and aspirations of your target audience. Your goal is more than just to entertain them. It is to connect and resonate on a personal level by showing how you have navigated similar challenges. You are not just a vendor but a fellow traveler and guide.

The Power of Collecting Stories

Now, let's talk about collecting stories. This means being attentive and mindful of the moments and experiences that surround you daily. These stories could come from your own life, interactions with customers, or observations in your community. Every story has potential, whether it is a lesson learned, a challenge faced, or a moment of unexpected joy. Stay alert. Keep your eyes and ears open for story-worthy moments. It could be customer feedback, a challenge in your workday, or a personal achievement. Stories are everywhere. You just need to be ready to capture them.

Make it a habit to write down these stories. Use your phone, a notebook, or whatever works best for you. The key is to capture the essence while it's fresh so you have a treasure trove of narratives to draw from when needed. Connect the dots. Every story should tie back to a concept or a message that you want to convey about your brand, business, or life. It is not just storytelling for the sake of it. Each story or narrative should reinforce your brand values, mission, and customer promise.

As I said, you can use them when needed. I use them a lot. For example, when I have a presentation and need to collect stories, I go back to my notes and try to select one that ties back to the concept or message that I'm talking about. I learned this from my mentor. I was fortunate to attend a seminar by John Zimmer, a world champion of public speaking. His presentations were not just informative but truly captivating. Each concept he shared was woven into a compelling story, making abstract ideas feel real and relatable. After the seminar, I reached out to him to be my mentor. We've had a couple of sessions, and he's been instrumental in teaching me how to leverage storytelling to clarify concepts, stir emotions, and reinforce messages. I'm grateful to him for this amazing lesson and for the moment that we connected.

In summary, your personal story is much more than a marketing tool. It is the soul of your brand. It is a testament to your journey, your values, and the impact you aim to make in the world. A 2015 study by Headstream provides additional evidence of the persuasive power of storytelling. According to this research, "if people love a brand story, 55% are more likely to buy the product in future, 44% will share the story, and 15% will buy the product immediately."

By mastering the art of storytelling and making your narrative resonate with your audience, you are not just building a brand; you are building a community.

"Stories are remembered up to 22 times more than facts alone."
–Jennifer Aaker

Designing Your Brand Message

Crafting your brand message is like setting the stage for a grand performance. It's about ensuring every word and every image aligns perfectly to tell the world who you are, what you stand for, why it matters, and why they should listen to you. This section will guide you through important steps to craft your message that resonates, connects, and converts.

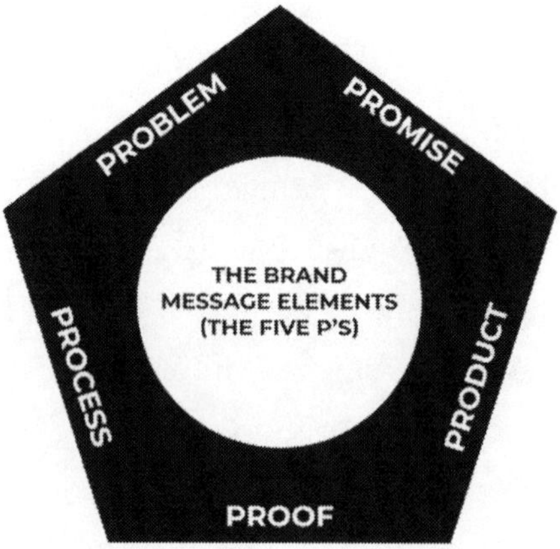

1. **Clarify the problem.** Your brand exists to solve a problem, to fill a gap, to make life better, easier, or more enjoyable in some way. Start by pinpointing the top three problems your business tackles. These should be the big issues that your target audience wrestles with all the time, the kind that keeps them searching for solutions, possibly even in the middle of the night. Your brand's job is to be the light at the end of the tunnel.
2. **Make a promise.** For every problem, there is a promise. This is where you get to shine, showcasing how your product or service not only addresses the issue but does so in a way that's unique to your brand. These promises are your pledge to your customers, the commitment that sets you apart from the crowd. They are not just features or benefits; they are transformative. They are the transformation your customers expect to experience or want to get.
3. **Highlight your product.** Your products or services are the heroes of your brand story. They are the tools, the solutions, the magic wands that make the promises come true. Detail the main offerings of your brand, focusing on how they specifically solve the problems you have identified. It's about connecting the dots for your customer, making it crystal clear how choosing your brand will change their story for the better.
4. **Showcase the proof.** Proof is your brand's backbone. It's the testimonial, the case studies, the before-and-after photos, everything that shows your brand in action and making good on its promises. This is where trust is built. It's one thing to claim you can solve a problem; it's another to show it. Gather your best evidence, certificates, testimonials, and the most compelling stories of transformation, and put them front and center.
5. **Outline the process.** Finally, walk your customers through how they will engage with your brand. From the first click to the final solution, this process should be as simple and transparent as possible,

removing any barriers or confusion that might stand in the way of a decision. Think of it as laying down a red carpet and inviting your customers to step into the world of your brand with confidence and excitement.

With these elements in place—problem, promise, product, proof, and process—your brand message becomes a powerful tool. It's not just about what you say; it's about how you make people feel. It's about creating a narrative people want to be part of that aligns with their desires, challenges, and inspirations.

Take Dove's "Campaign for Real Beauty" as a prime example. It wasn't just about selling soap or beauty products. It was about challenging and redefining beauty standards, making a promise that resonated deeply with their audience. This campaign showed how a well-crafted brand message could touch hearts, change minds, and, yes, even sell products. Dove's "Real Beauty Sketches," one part of the campaign, became particularly famous, reaching 163 million global views on YouTube. This campaign highlighted how women viewed themselves versus how others saw them, emphasizing the gap between self-perception and external perceptions of beauty.

Overall, the Dove "Campaign for Real Beauty" significantly impacted the beauty industry by promoting inclusivity and challenging traditional beauty standards. It helped reshape perceptions by featuring women of all ages, shapes, and sizes and focusing on inner beauty, self-esteem, and the diversity of natural beauty.

If you have a brand message in front of you, you will have a guiding force for your marketing, sales, and campaigns. It will also provide clarity for you to see how you transform lives. You can edit it when needed. Your brand message is your handshake, your first impression, and your promise to the world. Craft it with care, infuse it with authenticity, and watch as it opens doors, builds bridges, and creates lasting connections with your customers.

"Marketing is no longer about the stuff that you make, but about the stories you tell."
–Seth Godin

Understanding Why Customers Buy

Unlocking the mystery of why customers make a purchase is like discovering the secret ingredient to a master chef's signature dish. It's about understanding the deeper motivation behind their choices and how your brand can fulfill those needs. This section dives into the core reasons behind customers' decisions and how you can effectively align your offers to meet these desires.

As I said, I studied positive psychology and customer behaviors. I like to link both because when you build a business for people, you need to understand how people tick.

Designing for the Job to Be Done

Think of your product or service as being used by your customers to perform a specific job. This concept (Designing for the Job to Be Done) is inspired by the insights of authors Clayton M. Christensen, Taddy Hall, Karen Dillon, and David S. Duncan in their book *Competing Against Luck*. It shifts our focus from the product to the outcome it delivers. Every purchase is driven by a desire to accomplish something, whether it's to save time, reduce effort, enhance status, or provide comfort.

Bain & Company partnered with online sampling and data collection company D-NATA (formerly Research Now) to survey over 10,000 customers in the US. Based on that, they derived the elements of the value pyramid, which represent why people pay, including functional needs and social impact. To innovate and succeed, it's crucial to align your offering with the jobs your customers need to be done. This alignment requires a deep understanding of their goals, the challenges they face, and the context in which they use your product.

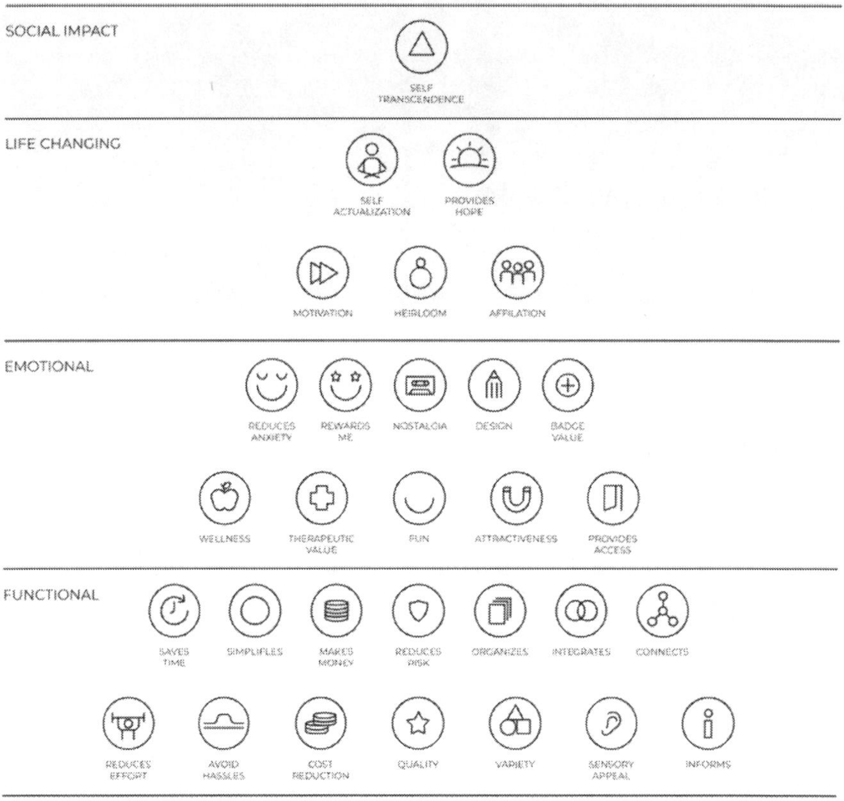

By analyzing customer behavior and feedback, you can tailor your product and services to fit seamlessly into their lives, making your brand part of their daily routines. When communicating with your customers, emphasize how your product or services make their lives better. It's not just about the features or the price. It's about the benefits and the outcomes they can expect, whether it's helping them save money, simplify complex ideas, or providing a sense of organization and control.

Make sure these benefits are front and center in your message, and use the elements of the value pyramid to highlight which of those promises you can use in your brand message. Understanding why customers make purchases comes from peeling back the layers to reveal the core motivations driving their decisions. By focusing on the jobs to be done—aligning your offers with customers' goals and emphasizing the benefits and outcomes of your products—you can create a compelling reason for customers to choose your brand or products. Remember, successful innovation is rooted in a deep understanding of customer needs and a commitment to meeting those needs in the most effective, authentic, and satisfying way possible.

Exercise:

Choose at least five reasons your customers should purchase your products from the value pyramid.

____

____

____

____

____

____

____

____

____

The Power of Seven—Surrounding Yourself With Support and Success

When I was thinking about starting my own business, I felt stuck. I was worried that my ideas weren't unique enough. Then, I got some advice from my mentor, a visiting professor at Oxford University. He told me something that really stuck with me. He said, "It's not always about having brand-new ideas. It's about how you put those ideas together and how you help your clients transform. That is what makes you stand out." This advice changed everything for me. It helped me see that I didn't need to be afraid of not being unique. Instead, I needed to focus on how I could help people in my own unique way.

This is an excellent example of how having the right people to guide you can really make a big difference in your life and work. On the entrepreneurial journey, the company you keep can significantly influence your path and outcomes. Embracing the concept of the "Power of Seven" is about strategically surrounding yourself with people who not only support your vision but also enrich your personal and professional growth.

The following seven groups of people bring diverse strengths and perspectives, acting as catalysts for your development and brand success.

1. **Unconditional Supporters:** These are the people who believe in you no matter what. Their unwavering faith in your abilities provides a safety net, allowing you to take risks and push boundaries with the knowledge that they have your back.
2. **Motivators and Encouragers:** This group consists of those who inspire and push you to go further. They are the cheerleaders on your entrepreneurial journey, celebrating your victories and encouraging you to persevere through challenges.
3. **Showcasers:** These people amplify your achievements, showcasing your strength and success to a broader audience. Their endorsement adds credibility and visibility to your followers and customers.
4. **Experienced Guides:** Having a mentor or advisor who has walked the path before you is invaluable. They offer wisdom, guidance, and often different perspectives that can help you navigate the complexity of entrepreneurship.
5. **Skill Enhancers:** Continuous learning and growth are key in the ever-evolving business landscape. Associating with people who can teach you new skills or enhance your existing ones ensures you stay relevant and competitive.
6. **Brand Amplifiers:** Just by associating with you, these collaborators or partners strengthen the presence of your business brand and your personal brand as well.
7. **Wise Elders:** These are the people, usually outside your industry, who offer timeless wisdom and grounding. Their broad, life-spanning insight can provide clarity and direction during moments of uncertainty and decision-making.

I have plenty of mentors, and I recommend cultivating relationships with people who are successful in their careers because they will give you wisdom when you turn to them. Building and nurturing these relationships is not a passive process. It requires intentional effort, mutual respect, and understanding that these connections are not merely for success but are also important to your well-being.

As you develop your brand and business, remember the immense value these seven types of relationships bring. You might find that one person actually has two or three characteristics of the seven that we have mentioned. Their collective influence can propel you toward your goals and help you navigate the entrepreneurial landscape with confidence and support.

Conclusion

Chapter 4 was all about turning your vision into reality.

We have laid out our plans on the one-page product canvas and connected deeply with our audience through our personal stories. We have honed our brand message to resonate clearly and crafted our offerings to meet the true needs of our customers, understanding the deeper reasons behind their choices. Most importantly, we have surrounded ourselves with mentors, motivators, and allies who push us to be our best.

As we gear up for the next phase, it's time to take action. Armed with our well-crafted products and having combined them with a story, we are ready to make a real impact. Let's move forward with confidence, bringing our unique contribution to the world. The act phase waits, and it's our time to make a unique contribution to the world.

Exercise:

Write down the names of the powerful individuals who will surround you on your journey.

CHAPTER 5

Act: Marketing and Sales Mastery

"The best marketing doesn't feel like marketing."
– Tom Fishburne

In Chapter 5, we reach the final stage of the **IdentityBrand Cycle**, where we are set to act and share our vision with the world. It's similar to beginning the drilling process in the oil and gas industry, but here, the real value lies in the learning that unfolds as we execute our plans. This continuous learning might reveal more about our brand or lead to new product ideas, thereby keeping the cycle of entrepreneurship growth in motion.

As we dive into the ACT phase, we will explore how to effectively communicate your brand's message, including strategies for engaging with audiences on social media. This chapter is about putting your ideas into action and embracing the lessons learned along the way to refine and evolve your brand continuously. Let's begin this journey of action, discovery, and growth.

Marketing and Sales Myths

Let's address some common misconceptions about marketing and sales. Many people believe that to succeed in these fields, you have to be deceptive or use manipulative tactics. This reputation has made many of us feel uneasy about engaging in marketing or sales. Many clients tell me that they hate marketing and sales. Usually, it's because they have limiting beliefs and misconceptions about them. However, a different approach can be taken.

When building my sales and marketing team, I decided to choose people who were more knowledgeable in coaching than in selling. They were passionate about helping people, not just making sales. We all agreed that our job was not to push products but to assist people in making decisions that were right for them.

This small change had a significant impact. For the last five years, we have received almost no complaints about our marketing and sales strategies, and our sales conversion rate has increased from 15% to 25% on average. When we shifted our focus from selling to helping, everything changed. Our hearts and minds opened up.

This section is not about using sales tricks. Instead, it's about viewing marketing and sales as tools to assist others. When you adopt this approach, you not only feel better about your work, but you also begin to enjoy it.

The Markemeter Approach

All right, let's dive into something I like to call the **Markemeter Approach**. For many, marketing can seem like a black hole, mysterious and a bit intimidating. However, as someone with a master's degree in organic geochemistry, I see marketing as more of a scientific process. It's not just throwing things out there and hoping for the best. It's about having the right ingredients and understanding the time of reaction.

1. **Understanding your brand message:** First thing first, let's talk about your brand message. Remember that we covered this in the previous chapter. Jumping into social media without a clue about your niche or what problems you're solving is like drilling for a well while blindfolded and hoping you strike it rich. You need a clear, compelling brand message as your starting point that tells everyone who you are and what you stand for.
2. **Crafting your offer:** Next up is your offer. And I'm not just talking about your product itself. It's about how you present it—with urgency, scarcity, social proof, and a clear process of how customers can engage with your solution to their problem. Think of it as setting up a storefront that's so inviting that people can't help but walk in and see what you've got.
3. **Attracting leads:** How do you get people to notice your offer? That's where lead attractions come in. You can use webinars, PDFs, mini-courses, or even sweet discounts. The goal here is to gradually build awareness and trust so that when people are ready to solve their problems, you are the first person they think of.

4. **Email marketing and retargeting campaigns:** Then, there is the power of email marketing and retargeting campaigns. I remember when social media platforms went down for a few hours a couple of years ago, and guess what? My clients with solid email lists could still reach their audience. They actually sent plenty of messages, and they thanked me for advising them to build their email lists. Email lists might seem old school, but they are still one of the best tools for marketing.
5. **Social media strategy:** Of course, there is social media, but notice that this isn't the first step. If you jump onto social media without a clear message or a strategy to attract and nurture leads, you are setting yourself up for a challenging ride. Social media is a powerful tool, but it's most effective as part of a bigger plan.

Sales Funnel

The secret to making all these elements work together is your sales funnel. It's like a flow chart that guides you through each step of the process. Engineers and project managers use similar techniques, so why not us?

Where to start? It's about planning each step, from social posts to lead magnets, and then gradually transitioning to a conversion or purchase. Picture your sales funnel as a journey map.

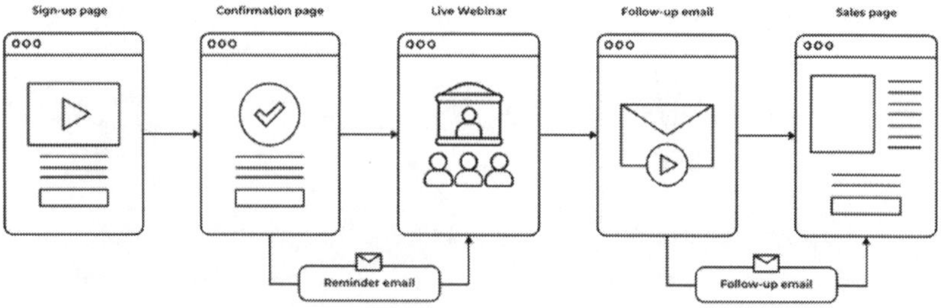

You start with a wide entrance where people first encounter your brand, maybe through a catchy social media post, paid ads, or a helpful blog article.

This is your chance to grab their attention and get them interested. From there, you lead them to the next stage with a lead magnet. Think of it as a small gift, an ebook, a discount code, or a free mini-course. It's your way of saying, "Hey, stick around. I have more to share because I care."

But the journey doesn't stop there. Next up might be an engaging webinar or an in-depth guide that dives deeper into the problem they are facing. This is where you build trust and establish yourself as a go-to expert in your field.

Now, here's where it gets exciting. After you have nurtured that relationship, and sometimes, it takes time—some people say it takes 40 to 50 touch points to build this trust—you gently guide them towards making a decision. This could be through a well-crafted sales page or your sales theme, which highlights the value of your offer and includes a strong call to action.

Remember, the funnel isn't just about leading people to sales. It's about creating a smooth, enjoyable journey for them. It's about making each step feel natural and exciting so that by the time they are ready to buy, it feels like the most obvious next step to them. And the funnel doesn't end at the sale. The final, crucial part is turning those customers into loyal fans by attaching a fulfillment funnel to your sales. This could mean emails, special offers for repeat customers, or a community where they can engage with you and other customers.

I recommend using different tools to build your sales funnels, but the most important is your pen and paper. Try to make it more visual. There's no right or wrong, but try to map your customer journey because this will help you not only understand where the leaky points are but also how to mix the ingredients of marketing successfully.

In summary, the **Markemeter Approach** is about randomly trying things and hoping they stick. It's a calculated, scientific approach to marketing, where every element has its place and every action has a purpose. It's about understanding the actions your marketing efforts will provoke and using that knowledge to build a marketing strategy that is effective and enjoyable to execute.

Setting Measurable KPIs

As a business owner, it's important to set measurable Key Performance Indicators (KPIs) to assess the effectiveness of your marketing and sales efforts. KPIs act as a guide to your strategy and provide insights into what's working and what needs tweaking.

Let's take a closer look at my top five favorite key metrics that every business owner or entrepreneur should monitor.

1. **Revenue and expense tracking:** Keep a close eye on your monthly and weekly revenue against your overheads. This will give you a clear picture of your financial health, which is very important, as you know. If possible, highlight trends, forecast future performance, and identify areas where costs can be optimized without compromising quality.
2. **Lead generation metrics:** Monitor the growth of your email list or the number of leads generated through various channels. This could be the number of messages, the number of new people interested in your product or service, or the number of people asking about your product and services. Try to select what metrics you can use to track your leads. This metric is crucial because it indicates the effectiveness of your lead magnets if you have them and initiates customer engagement strategies.
3. **Conversion rates:** Pay attention to how well your website or sales team converts leads into buying customers. A healthy conversion rate meets your sales funnel and effectively guides potential customers through their journey from initial interest to final purchase.
4. **Value delivery:** Quantify the value you provide each month, such as the number of posts, videos, webinars, or any other content you create. This is one of the metrics that I really love. It's not everywhere.

I don't see it a lot in books or marketing sales webinars, but it's very important because, at the end of the day, you are the guide. Think about the value—and to think about it, you need to measure it. It's one of the most important metrics that I keep an eye on. This metric isn't just about the volume; it's about the consistent delivery of quality content that educates, engages, and enriches your audience.

5. **Customer lifetime value:** Understanding customer lifetime value is crucial for long-term success. It's not just about initial sales but the total value a customer brings to the relationship with your brand. It helps in creating upsells, cross-sells, and loyalty programs. For instance, acquiring a customer might cost you $200, but if they end up purchasing products or services worth $1,600 over time, the investment is well worth it.

Setting and monitoring these KPIs allows you to make data-driven decisions, ensuring your marketing and sales strategies align with your business goals. They offer a clear insight into where to allocate resources for maximum impact and where to adjust your approach for better results.

Remember, the key to effective KPI tracking is consistency and the willingness to adapt based on what the data tells you.

Dealing with Social Media

Navigating social media can be challenging. You need to find the right balance between professionalism and personal touch. In this section, we will explore strategies that can help you enhance your social media presence and make your brand truly heard and felt.

- **Authenticity and credibility** are crucial for building a strong online presence. In a world where so much content is available, being genuine and transparent can make you stand out. You should showcase what makes your brand unique and share your story. Authenticity builds trust, which is essential for creating long-lasting relationships. Sharing a human side of your brand, such as behind-the-scenes glimpses, real customer stories, or your brand's journey, can help you connect with your customers.

- **Sharing personal stories** can help you connect with your audience. Your brand story isn't just a narrative; it's a way to connect with your followers and make your brand more relatable. Sharing your journey, the challenges you have faced, and the successes you have celebrated can make your brand more human and help you connect with your audience on a deeper level. Your notebook of personal and brand stories will be helpful in this stage.
- **Video content is essential.** Videos can be very engaging and can educate and entertain your customers. You can create short or long videos. Based on much research, people engage more with videos than text and retain the information better.
- **Volume and consistency** are key when it comes to social media. Establish a regular posting schedule to keep your audience engaged and your brand at the top of their minds. However, it's not just about quantity. You should also make sure that every piece of content aligns with your brand message and values.
- **Becoming an expert** in your niche can help you attract a dedicated following. You can share your knowledge through in-depth guides, webinars, or case studies. Engaging with industrial leaders and sharing your insights and opinions on current trends can also help you build credibility and turn your social media platforms into go-to resources for valuable information. Yes, I know that many people don't like to be confined to a niche and feel it is constraining. However, being specialized at something and positioning yourself as an expert in one field, especially at the beginning, is very important because you filter down to your ideal customers and establish yourself as a go-to person for that niche or idea.

The Art and Science of Artificial Intelligence (AI)

AI is a new tool to work with, and it's now being used for everything from crafting and compiling copy to designing sophisticated software and reshaping marketing and sales strategies. It's an exciting time to harness the power of AI to elevate your brand and save you time and effort. With the vast array of technological tools at our disposal, it's crucial to tread carefully to avoid getting overwhelmed.

As we integrate AI into our workflows, the key is to stay focused on what truly benefits our brand. It's easy to get caught up in the latest tech craze, but only some tools will align with your goals. Regularly revisit your sales and marketing funnels and identify areas where AI can make a real impact, whether it's automating customer service inquiries, personalizing marketing messages, or choosing tools that streamline your operations and enhance your customer interactions.

Select your tools wisely. With the diversity of AI tools available, take the time to evaluate what each offers and how it fits into your existing strategy.

It's not just about adopting AI for the sake of innovation. It's about integrating technology that complements and amplifies your brand's message and values.

62% of consumers say they are less likely to engage with and trust content if they know it was created by an AI application.

(Source: Hootsuite Social Trends 2024 consumer Survey)

(*This is why I recommend you maintain a balance between AI and your own identity.)

Carol Dweck, one of the leading psychiatrists in the field of positive psychology and author of *Mindset: The New Psychology of Success*, emphasizes that embracing a growth mindset is essential when navigating anything, including AI. By fostering a mindset that welcomes challenge and innovation, we become better equipped to adapt to the evolving digital ecosystem.

AI presents a world of opportunities for marketing and sales, offering unprecedented ways to connect with and understand our customers. By staying focused, choosing the right tools for our brand, and maintaining a growth mindset, we can leverage AI to not just keep up with the trends but to lead them.

As we come to the end of the chapter and the journey through the **IdentityBrand Cycle**, the main takeaway is the power of motion. Everything is in motion. The cycle never ends. It evolves. Each step in the cycle, from dreaming to defining, designing to acting, enriches your understanding of your brand and yourself. With every round, you gain fresh insights, encounter different challenges, and uncover new opportunities. This continuous loop is not just about refining your brand; it's also about personal growth and expanding your mindset. The journey transforms you from a dreamer with an idea to a giver with a mission. Each phase of the cycle equips you with new tools, insights, and experience, enabling you to contribute more profoundly to your customers' lives and the broader community.

Embracing this never-ending cycle means embracing a journey of consistent discovery and reinvention. It's about staying curious, being open to change, and always being willing to learn. The **IdentityBrand Cycle** isn't just a pathway to building a successful brand; it's a roadmap for lifelong learning and growth.

Conclusion

The end of this cycle is just the beginning of a new phase, a new cycle. Keep cycling, keep learning, and keep growing. Your journey from dreamer to giver is an ongoing adventure filled with endless possibilities and opportunities to make a lasting impact in this world.

Exercise:

Identify one element of the **Markemeter Approach** that requires development and outline three actionable steps to strengthen it.

CHAPTER 6

The Six Pillars of Entrepreneurial Success

"You can't manage what you don't measure."
– Unknown

As an entrepreneur, it's important to strike a balance between your professional and personal lives to achieve success and, most importantly, maintain momentum. This is crucial not only for the longevity of your business but also for your satisfaction and fulfillment. To achieve this balance between life and business and ensure continuous growth, we need to focus on six essential pillars.

I often share these pillars with my clients, and I call them pillars because they are the foundation for achieving fulfillment, success, and growth in your business and life. You can also call them Key Performance Indicators (KPIs), but I like to call them pillars. The pillars are tailored for both personal development and business excellence.

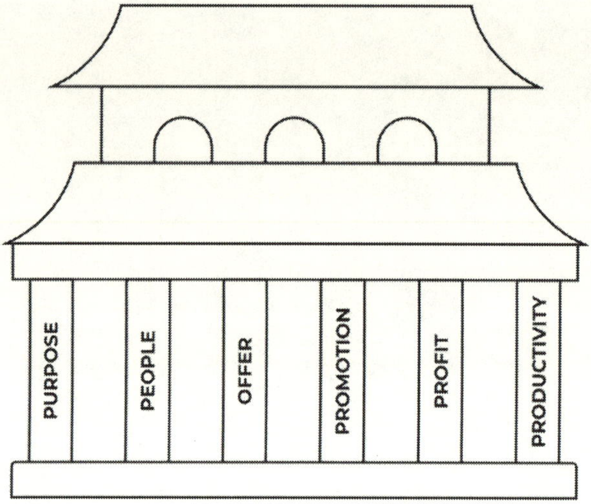

Pillar One: Your Purpose

The first pillar is your purpose, the guiding light that keeps you driven and generous, especially during challenging times. To keep this flame alive, consider the three critical aspects:

1. **Brand message alignment:** It's important to regularly review your brand message and make sure it still aligns with your core motivations and your VSP. Your brand message should inspire and energize you. If it no longer does that, it's time to refresh it and give it another look. You can adjust the wording or the phrases to reignite the initial inspiration while ensuring that it reflects your current ambition and deep values.
2. **Deepening your why:** A crucial aspect of maintaining your drive and purpose is connecting with your deep why, the core reason that motivates you. This is about more than just aligning your actions with your business's vision, strategy, and plan. It's about ensuring you have a profound personal connection with what you do every day. This could stem from various sources that are significant to you, such as family members, legacy, or spiritual beliefs. The essence here

isn't about how others perceive you but what has internal value to you. Sometimes, we receive unexpected yet affirming messages that can be considered from a higher power, such as the universe, God, or Allah. These messages can remind us of the impact of our work when we are questioning our journey and the fruits of our labor. At times, I receive unexpected messages from clients, some from years past, expressing gratitude for advice or tools I shared during challenging times. Such moments reassure us that our efforts have significance. They are not mere coincidences; they are timely reminders that staying committed to our purpose will guide us toward the transformative results we seek to achieve.

3. **Winning habits:** According to a study cited in Charles Duhigg's *The Power of Habit: Why We Do What We Do in Life and Business*, over 40% of our daily actions are habitual rather than deliberate choices. Sustaining your purpose requires embedding winning habits into your daily routine. These habits should resonate with your VSP and enrich your personal and professional lives. For instance, immersing yourself in nature or taking up a new physical activity annually can ignite your purpose. It's about finding activities that resonate personally with you. Drawing from conversations with numerous successful entrepreneurs, I've compiled a list of 30 habits for you to use to find and commit to ones that best align with your essence.

Pillar Two: People

In the journey of building a successful and fulfilling business, the way we interact and nurture relationships with people, be they customers, support groups, or team members, is paramount.

Let's explore three key areas to focus on to strengthen this pillar:

1. **Ideal Customer:** Understanding and connecting with your ideal customer is the cornerstone of any business. By rigorously revisiting and reaffirming them, you're refining your customer profile, ensuring your marketing and sales efforts are targeted and effective. Engage in surveys and evaluations to gauge the impact of your offerings and gather insights. This continuous feedback loop not only enhances your marketing and sales but, more importantly, fosters trust between you and your customers. It's about building a relationship where customers feel heard and valued, paving the way for long-term loyalty and trust.
2. **Support Group Dynamics:** Reflect on your support network, the "Power of 7," which encompasses mentors, peers, and partners who contribute to your personal and professional growth. Periodically assess the strength and value of these relationships. Are they fulfilling and reciprocal? Is there room for expansion or a need for realignment? A robust support system not only offers guidance and encouragement but also challenges you to stretch your limits and explore new perspectives.
3. **Team Members:** Your team is the engine of your business. Ensuring your team is aligned with and embodies the brand's values is critical. Regular check-ins and open communication channels can reinforce a shared vision and collective commitment. Evaluate whether everyone is on the same page and moving towards a common goal. Team dynamics can significantly influence the internal culture and, by extension, the customer experience. Cultivating a positive, supportive, and aligned team environment is essential for sustained growth and success.

Strengthening the people pillar involves a continuous and conscious effort to ensure and develop the relationships that form the foundation of your business. You can build a resilient framework that supports scaling and long-term fulfillment by maintaining a clear focus on your ideal customers, fostering a supportive and engaging network, and ensuring team alignment.

Pillar Three: Perfecting Your Core Offer

In the business growth journey, the third pillar to strengthen is the core product and the strategies employed for its promotion, development, and packaging. Mastering this pillar is crucial to ensure that your offers not only meet market demands but stand out in a competitive landscape.

There are three elements to strengthening this pillar.

1. **Strong core product:** The foundation of your business lies in a core product that effectively addresses a specific problem, offering a solution that customers are willing to invest their time and money in. This product should be the result of a deep understanding of your customers' needs and crafted to deliver tangible benefits. Focus on perfecting this product before expanding your portfolio. Continual development and process automation for this core offering ensure that you maintain quality and consistency, which are key factors in building customer trust and loyalty.
2. **Packaging with love:** There needs to be more than just a product to capture the market's attention. Robert Cialdini is an American psychologist known for his work on the psychology of persuasion and marketing. He created the "7 Principles of Influence (or Persuasion)"—reciprocity, commitment or consistency, consensus or social proof, authority, liking, scarcity, and unity. We want to draw from his principles and incorporate elements of urgency, social proof, and scarcity into your offering. This approach not only enhances the product's appeal but also encourages prompt action from potential customers. Ethical use of these principles is important. They should be used to genuinely assist customers in making decisions that are beneficial for them. Think creatively about how you can integrate these elements to make sure your offer is irresistible.

3. **Put it together with a Simple Landing Page:** In today's digital age, presenting your product and offer effectively requires a user-friendly website. With numerous tools and platforms available, creating a compelling online presence is both affordable and straightforward. A well-designed website serves as a testament to your professionalism and commitment, providing a platform where customers can learn about your offerings, understand their value, and take the next step in engaging with your brand. By continually innovating and refining your product offer cycle, you position your business as a leader in your industry. This proactive approach to product development and marketing ensures that you remain a step ahead of competitors, consistently delivering value that resonates with your audience and fosters sustainable growth.

Pillar Four: Promotion

In the continuously evolving world of marketing, promotion is a crucial pillar for establishing trust, building impact, and increasing profit. To ensure that your promotional efforts are effective and aligned with your brand's message, focus on the following three essential elements:

1. **Core marketing channels:** In the digital age, there are many digital channels to choose from, which can be overwhelming. Concentrate on one or two channels initially instead of spreading yourself over many of them. Choose a platform based on where your target customers are. For instance, LinkedIn is great for engaging with professionals, while TikTok and Instagram are more suited for younger demographics. Focus enables you to maintain a strong presence and connect meaningfully with your audience.
2. **Lead generation:** Lead generation is a critical aspect of your marketing strategy that requires consistent attention. It's not just about quantity but also the quality of leads and the cost-effectiveness of acquiring them. Experiment with various tools and methods to

find what works best for your brand, and be patient. Building a robust lead generation system takes some time, but it pays off in the long run by ensuring a steady stream of potential customers.

3. **Promoting your Philosophy, Value, and Offer (PVO):** A common question from my customers is what to promote on social media. The answer lies in your PVO, your brand's philosophy, value, and offer. Your philosophy sets you apart, showing customers why your brand is unique. Sharing valuable content that answers questions, provides tips, or offers insight helps build trust with your audience. Of course, remember to promote your offers. Showing your products or services is essential. Aim for a balance where the majority of your content revolves around your philosophy and value, with a strategic emphasis on your offers.

As you navigate the promotional landscape, maintain authenticity in all your communications. Remember, your role is to guide and serve your audience, not just to sell to them. Authentic promotion resonates more deeply with customers, fostering a sense of trust and reality that goes beyond transactional interactions.

Concentrating on these key elements of the promotional pillar can create a powerful strategy that raises awareness of your brand and cultivates a loyal community of customers who believe in what you stand for.

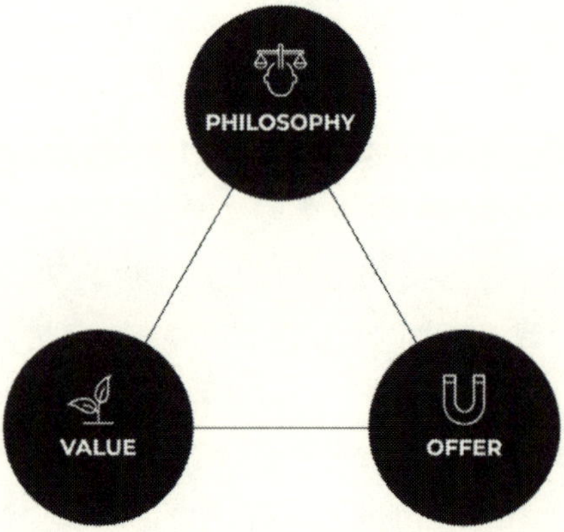

Pillar Five: Profit

Profit is often a challenging subject. It's common for some to feel hesitant about asking for money, perhaps due to a lack of confidence in their product or its impact. However, embracing a win-win mindset is crucial for success, and confidence encapsulates this well. If you are poor, it's hard to serve the poor. This implies that achieving financial success isn't about greed. It is about enabling yourself to serve others more effectively.

Three key elements can strengthen your profit pillar:

1. **Define your financial goals:** Start by setting clear financial goals. Reverse-engineer these goals to understand what needs to be accomplished daily, monthly, quarterly, and annually. Regular check-ins, either with your team or even with a spouse or partner, help you maintain focus and motivation toward these goals.
2. **Monitor conversion rates:** Your conversion rate, the ratio of customers to leads, is a vital metric in understanding the health of your profit pillar. By tracking and analyzing this rate, you can pinpoint areas that need improvement and implement strategies to enhance profitability.
3. **Profit-enhancing habits:** Just as there are habits that fuel our purpose, there are habits that directly influence our profit. For me, engaging in sports, meditation, and investing have been vital. Although sports and nature may not seem directly related to financial gain, they significantly enhance my mood and effectiveness in managing my team and serving customers, ultimately contributing to profitability. This positive energy translates into better business outcomes and decisions.

Investing, on the other hand, is a more direct way to increase profit. Diversifying my portfolio with stock shares or investing in startups not only enhances my financial standing but also broadens my understanding of various market dynamics. This knowledge is invaluable in attaining insights as a businessman and enabling me to make more informed decisions.

Incorporating these profit-enhancing habits into your routine can have a significant impact on your business's bottom line. It's about finding those activities that resonate with you personally and align with your business goals, thereby strengthening the profit pillar of your enterprise or startup.

By re-evaluating and strengthening this pillar, you can transform your business and personal life. Maintain a clear perspective on the importance of profit and the role it plays in enabling you to serve and succeed. Keep this pillar in sharp focus and continuously nurture it for sustained growth and impact.

Pillar Six: Productivity

Productivity is the primary key to success because it helps you make the most of your time. One of my mentors asked me how I calculate my hours. This question alone was a turning point for me. I now base my decision to take on a task on the return on investment of my time and energy, whether financial or emotional.

There are three keys to strengthening this pillar:

1. **Master your calendar:** If you don't have a calendar for your tasks, habits, and other important events, you are missing an opportunity to double or triple your productivity. An empty slot on your calendar can easily be filled with many things or even nothing. It's important to keep an eye on your calendar and start with an ideal week to guide you. It's better to apply 60% than nothing at all.
2. **Build SOPs:** Building Standard Operating Procedures, or SOPs, for everyday tasks, can help you and your team avoid reinventing the wheel. For example, if you run a successful Facebook ad campaign, write down the steps you took or record them on a tool like Loom. Then, store what you've written as a reference for you or your team in the future. Recording SOPs on a weekly basis will help you and your team tackle tasks more efficiently.

3. **Automate using technology:** Technology is a blessing when it comes to speeding up and taking shortcuts for long tasks. Nowadays, you can create a sales funnel using AI and many other tools. It's important to use technology smartly to automate your SOPs and speed up the work, which can double your productivity. In my opinion, having a capturing tool to store ideas, like Todoist or Apple Notes, can free your mind from having to remember so it can focus on the most important thing, which is creating and being more creative.

Conclusion

The pillars as a whole represent the balanced approach necessary for long-term success. Let this chapter be your guide toward building a business that not only prospers financially but also enriches lives, including your own. Are you ready to take the next step? Let's move into Chapter 7, where we will discuss how to recharge and conquer your viruses.

Exercise:

Identify your top three foundational pillars that require strengthening and specify one actionable step for enhancing each pillar.

____

____

____

____

____

CHAPTER 7

The Art of Emotional Mastery in Entrepreneurship

"Out of suffering have emerged the strongest souls; the most massive characters are seared with scars."
– Khalil Gibran

According to a recent study by Small Business Silver Lining, which utilizes a tech-enabled, data-driven SaaS program rooted in behavior change science, 75% of small business owners are concerned about their mental health, with 56% having been diagnosed with anxiety, depression, or stress-related problems by a doctor or mental health professional. Therefore, it's essential to take care of your mental health and recharge to maintain your momentum. In this chapter, we will discuss the emotional journey of entrepreneurship, including how to navigate its ups and downs. We will explore the top five viruses that entrepreneurs typically encounter during their journey that can impact their momentum and meaning. We will also provide strategies for conquering these viruses every time. Lastly, we will dive into the source of happiness in business and your life.

The Emotional Journey of Entrepreneurship

Every entrepreneur, when pursuing their dream, will face a standard emotional journey. This journey was first introduced to me at a conference by Bill Gross, the founder of Idea Lab, who credited the noted tech entrepreneur, software engineer, and blogger John Saddington with the concept. The journey begins with a great idea and high energy. However, as we spend more time with our ideas, we realize the difficulties involved, and our enthusiasm decreases. Inevitably, we end up in the dark swamp of despair or doubt, the lowest point in a project where we consider quitting.

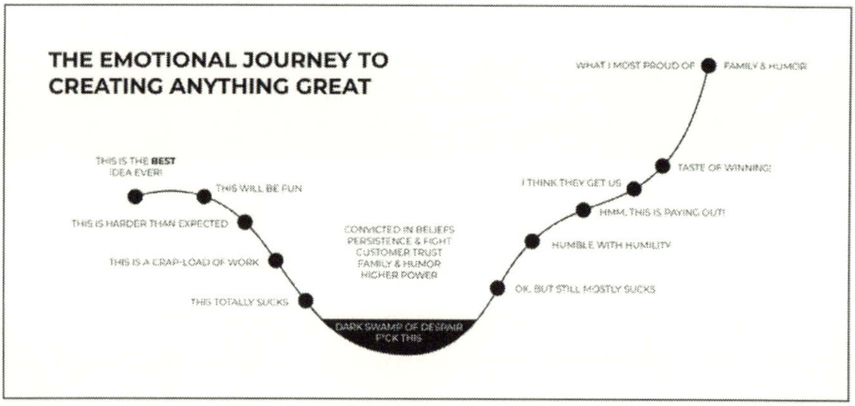

Unfortunately, this is where many people make the mistake of quitting and starting again. This is a mistake because we always think the new journey won't be like the previous one, but it ends up being the exact same journey, and we find ourselves working on yet another idea in no time. Thus begins our endless journey of searching for the perfect idea where we don't hit the door of doubt.

However, with the help of your support system and finding your why and meaning again, you can cross the swamp. The steps of the emotional journey are very close to the story structure we highlighted earlier. You start with a desire and momentum and then face challenging circumstances.

Sometimes, you reach the climax of the challenge, the swamp, where you face your fears.

By relying on your powers and support system, you can conquer your fear and start the transformation phase. This ends with the legacy stage, where you guide others to overcome their fears and cross their swamps. Thus, this journey will help you understand that all entrepreneurs, from Steve Jobs to Walt Disney, face the same journey. It's okay to feel down sometimes, but never give up. To cross your swamp of doubt, keep moving forward by aligning your VSP and surrounding yourself with the right people.

The Five Viruses and Their Antidotes

You will experience an emotional roller coaster during the journey. Most of the challenges will happen inside your mind and heart. Based on my work with thousands of entrepreneurs and my background as a positive psychology practitioner, I've identified five viruses that will come and go. You need to protect and immunize yourself from these viruses. Some will highly impact certain people based on their personality and values, so check which viruses affect you the most and get the vitamins to keep them in your toolkit.

Virus One: A Lack of Drive

Sometimes, you need to have a certain drive to keep moving forward and be consistent. This virus can hold you back from achieving your goals.

The three vitamins that you can use to conquer this virus are:

1. **Connect:** Think back to why you started your business or project and align it with your values, strengths, and passions.
2. **Plan:** Sometimes, we lose the drive because we don't know what to do. So, start small, think about what you can control, and create a plan of small actions that you can build upon.
3. **Inspire:** What sparks your motivation and inspires you? Try to ask for a partner or group to practice those activities with. These vitamins will help you get strong and overcome a lack of drive.

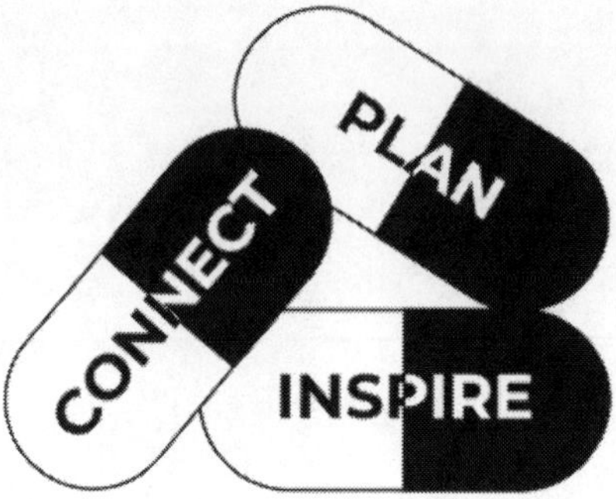

Virus Two: Fixed Mindset, or I Can't

One of the deadly viruses is a fixed mindset. A fixed mindset sees failures as disasters, while a growth mindset sees them as opportunities. People with a fixed mindset obstruct their development by believing in talent and fearing failure. On the other hand, people with a growth mindset work and train hard to realize their potential to the fullest. Ultimately, we can develop a growth mindset by confronting our attitudes and ideas, so be ready with these vitamins.

1. **Use the power of yet:** With a growth mindset, entrepreneurs focus on learning rather than just looking smart. They see effort as the key to success and thrive in the face of challenges. They know how to embrace the word "yet." So if you can't do things "yet," say it now, as this alone can change your perspective and mindset.
2. **Learn from the black dot:** Imagine a lousy situation that happened to you in the past and represent that as a black dot. Then, draw three lines stretching out from it. Those are the lessons you learned from the situation. For example, the first time I was on the stage was unpleasant, but because of that, I decided to study public speaking. I joined Toastmasters and became a member of the National Speakers Association. Imagine all the black dots that have taught you lessons. Do you still call them black dots?

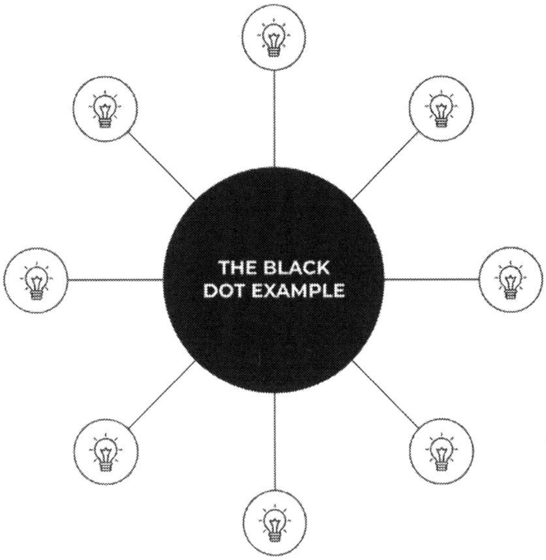

3. **Welcome challenges:** One of the few concepts that changed my mind is the power of welcoming challenges. Challenges are coming whether you are ready for them or not, but having a growth mindset will keep you smiling. Welcome challenges because they are opportunities to strengthen your mind and purify your heart.

"The greater the obstacle, the more glory in overcoming it."
–Molière

Virus Three: Perfectionism

Perfectionism is not the answer. Expecting or waiting for everything to be perfect can kill your confidence and make you feel insecure. Don't become a perfectionist. It's better to be 50% excellent and share your ideas with the world instead of waiting until you are 100% perfect and nothing is happening.

The three vitamins that can help you overcome this virus are:

1. **Be realistic:** Sometimes, entrepreneurs have unrealistic goals, which usually drive them to procrastinate more. If your mind is not ready

to burn calories for that job or task, then being realistic and straightforward with your goals will trick your mind and encourage you to start.

2. **Practice self-compassion:** Some entrepreneurs procrastinate, and then they go into a cycle of self-guilt and shame. Practicing self-compassion can be as simple as rewarding yourself with a cup of coffee after a challenging task, going on a vacation, or just enjoying a nice date. You can also practice self-compassion through compassionate letter writing: writing a letter to yourself as your best friend. It may sound strange, but try it and see the positive impact it has on your mindset.
3. **Celebrate:** Celebrate more of your small successes along your journey. These victories serve as stepping stones that ignite the spark necessary to maintain momentum and drive toward achieving your goals. Recognizing and appreciating even the smallest achievements can provide a sense of accomplishment and motivation to keep pushing forward, fostering a positive mindset and fueling progress in your pursuit of success. By acknowledging these incremental wins, you build resilience, confidence, and a strong foundation for reaching your ultimate objectives.

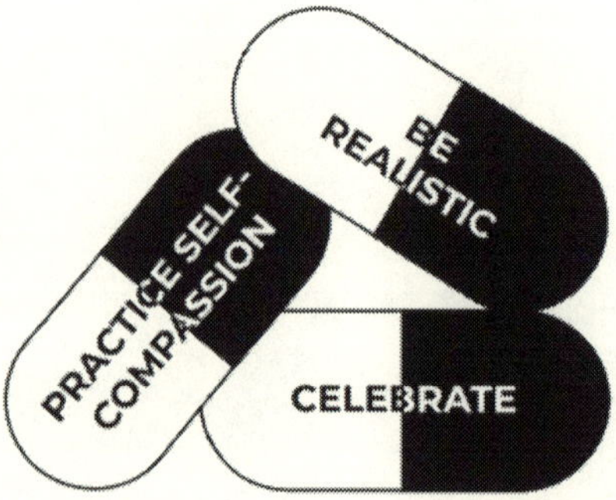

Virus Four: Lack of Self-Discipline

Self-discipline is the key to being your boss in the entrepreneurial world or life. One definition I like for self-discipline is that it is a mental ability that allows people to regulate their thoughts, emotions, and behavior to achieve their goals. So, as you can see, if you have no goals, there is no reason to be self-disciplined. Also, it's a mental ability, so it's something happening in your mind, not just a tool or strategy. It's the relationship between your goal and your mental ability.

The three vitamins to overcome this virus are:

1. **Set a routine:** A routine is a great way to develop self-discipline. Start by waking up at the same time every day. Then, set specific times for work, exercise, and relaxation. Performing these simple activities at set times can help build your self-discipline.
2. **Practice mindfulness:** Mindfulness involves focusing on the present moment with a heightened awareness of your thoughts and emotions. Through consistent mindfulness practice, you can gain deeper insights into your habitual patterns, leading to improved decision-making. This heightened self-awareness can foster greater self-discipline, empowering you to navigate challenges with resilience and clarity.
3. **Visualize success:** Visualizing success is a powerful technique that can significantly boost your motivation and discipline levels. Take a moment to vividly picture yourself successfully achieving your goals. Envision the details of the accomplishment and immerse yourself in the emotions of that moment. By mentally experiencing the taste of victory, you ignite a powerful drive within yourself that propels you forward, helping you overcome obstacles and stay focused on your path to success.

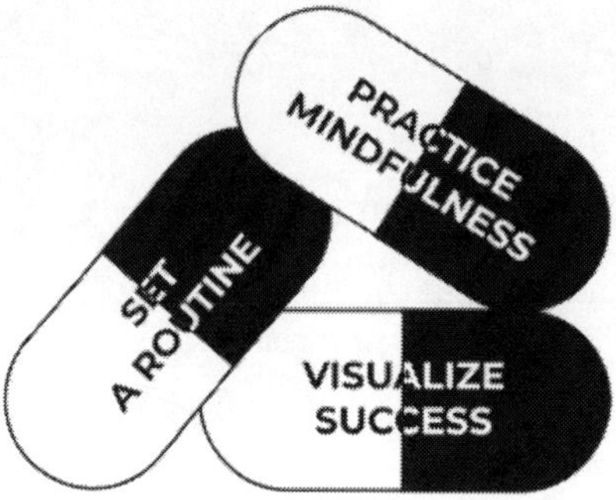

Virus Five: Fear

Each of us has a flavor of fear that matches our values, and it's okay to be afraid because we all are human. However, I'm referring to the fear that holds you back from achieving your dreams. This could be the fear of failure, rejection, or even success. But as Susan Jeffers said in her book *Feel the Fear and Do It Anyway*, the source of all fear is based on one general concern: not being able to handle what life throws at you.

Here are some vitamins that can help you conquer that bad fear:

1. **Take action:** Sometimes, the most effective method to conquer fear is to act in spite of it, as fear lingers until you take action. Additionally, when faced with fear, combating it with knowledge is key. This is known as the knowledge-confidence loop: the more you know, the greater your confidence grows, and as your confidence increases, your fear becomes more manageable.
2. **The power of now:** Studies by cognitive psychologist Stefan Van der Stigchel show that we spend a significant number of hours daydreaming—up to half of our day. Sometimes, that can lead to unhappiness and fear because our minds often run into the future or the past. Unfortunately, our human nature to avoid danger means we don't always expect the best. Therefore, it's essential to focus on now. Practicing mindfulness can help.

3. **Seek support:** Reaching out to friends, family members, or mentors can help you conquer your fears. Embrace the opportunity to invest in these networks and support groups starting today. Remember the power of seven.

Now, you have the vitamins you need to fight these viruses when you encounter them. Some of these viruses will be seasonal, and some will come more frequently based on your personality and values. Empower yourself with these vitamins and be ready because there are people who need you around. They need your special heart and authenticity to be a better person.

The Ancient Secret of Happiness

Happiness ultimately comes down to individual values. Everyone's path to happiness is unique and personal. While we all know what makes us happy, we must take action to achieve it. Rather than focusing solely on success, as our partners or society may have taught us, we should prioritize happiness as a critical aspect of our lives.

I have discovered that the path to happiness differs from the path to success. Research by acclaimed psychology professor Barbara Fredrickson (a psychology professor at the University of North Carolina) and others has shown that practicing happiness and experiencing positive emotions can build your physical, intellectual, social, and psychological resources, and this can lead to success. *So, the equation is different than many people think. Rather than success leading to happiness, it is happiness that leads to success.*

One way to better understand happiness is by applying the ten keys highlighted in Vanessa King's book, *10 Keys of Happier Living*:

- **Giving:** Do kind things for others.
- **Relating:** Connect with people.
- **Exercising:** Take care of your body.
- **Awareness:** Live mindfully.
- **Trying out:** Keep learning new things.
- **Direction:** Have goals to look forward to.
- **Resilience:** Find ways to bounce back.
- **Emotions:** Look for what's good.
- **Acceptance:** Be comfortable with who you are.
- **Meaning:** Be part of something bigger.

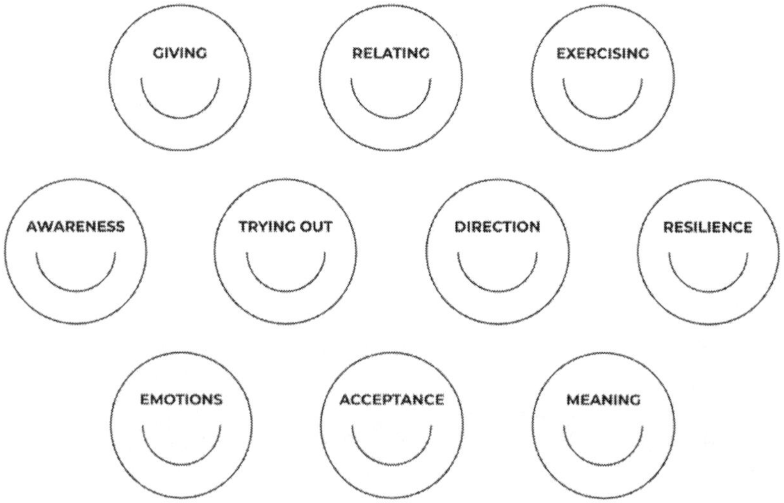

By implementing these concepts into our lives, we can come closer to achieving a happier life and enjoying the entrepreneurial journey. Remember, happiness is the goal, not success.

Prominent psychologist and researcher Dr. Hugo Alberts introduced the sailboat metaphor, which connects different aspects of human life with the components of a sailboat. It is often used as a coaching tool. The elements of the sailboat metaphor include the water, the compass, the steering wheel, the sails, other boats, the weather, leaks, and destinations.

- **The Water** represents the direct physical reality we live in and interact with. Sometimes, when we change jobs or our environment and still experience the same problems, the issue might not be the water but a leak in the boat, a weakness, or a limiting belief that we have. Therefore, before we change jobs or ideas, we need to ask ourselves whether the problem lies in the water or the boat.
- **The Compass** represents our experiences, such as feelings, emotions, and intuition. It serves as a tool for navigation and orientation and can provide both positive and negative data.
- **The Steering Wheel** represents our personal values and determines how we want to live our lives.
- **The Leaks**, as I said above, represent personal weaknesses that reduce our well-being. Weaknesses can manifest themselves at the physical, cognitive, or behavioral level.
- **The Sails** represent our strengths, which move us forward toward our values or destination. Even when we fix our leaks, sometimes, the boat will not move. We need to maximize our strengths and use the sails to keep the boat and our lives moving.
- **Other Boats** represent the values of the people around us and our relationships with them. Some people will help you in bad weather, and some can stand in the way of your destination. Sometimes, you just need to turn around and keep moving.
- **The Weather** can be compared to the events in our lives. Just as we cannot control the weather, positive and negative events will take place that we cannot control. Sometimes, the wind fills our sails, and we encounter situations that allow us to use our strengths optimally.

At other times, the wind and rain make it difficult to keep traveling in our perfect direction, but when we adopt a holistic perspective, we can just slow down and put our sails down.

- **Destinations** symbolize our goals and the deeper meaning behind our efforts. These goals guide our direction, motivating and enriching our journey with purpose. Each destination reflects our values and aspirations, marking significant milestones in our personal and professional growth.

By understanding and using these elements effectively, we can lead fulfilling and rewarding lives. We need to realize that every element in the boat is important to keep it sailing and to enjoy every minute of our journey.

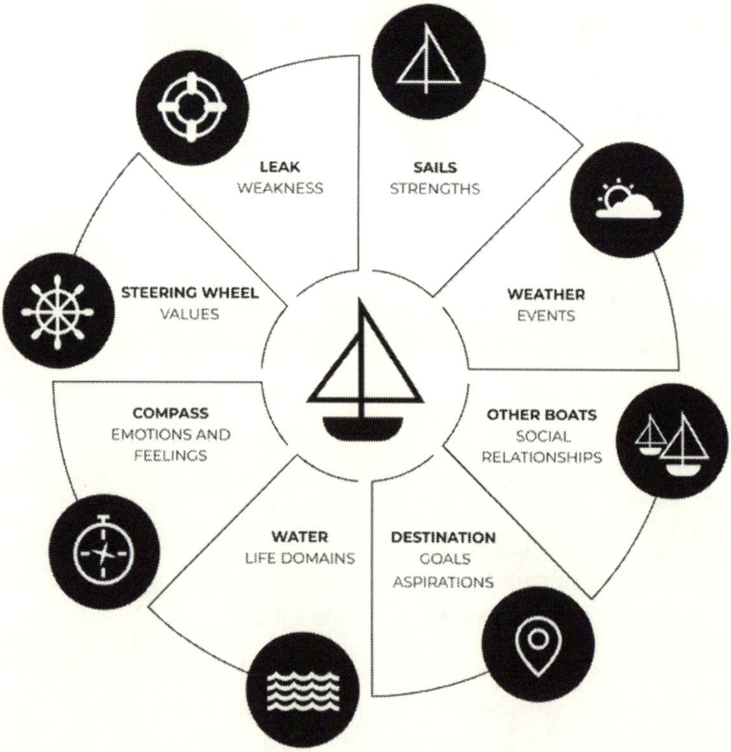

Conclusion

This chapter emphasized the intertwining path of happiness and success on the entrepreneur's journey. Understanding personal values, strengths, and the emotional rollercoaster of entrepreneurship is crucial. By embracing the sailboat metaphor, we learn to navigate life's waters with resilience, adaptability, and focus on well-being, recognizing that happiness and success are complementary and that happiness is the key to success and fulfillment in the entrepreneurial journey.

"Happiness is not by chance, but by choice."
–Jim Rohn

Exercise:

Antidote Reflection: What are the top 3 antidotes that you need to dial up more from now on to combat the common entrepreneurial viruses discussed?

____

____

____

____

____

____

____

____

Emotional Resilience Plan: Identify a time when you overcame one of the five "versus" (challenges) mentioned. What strategies did you employ, and how can you apply these lessons to future challenges?

Sailboat Metaphor Analysis: Reflect on the sailboat metaphor. Which element of the sailboat (e.g., the sails, the compass, or the leaks) do you need to pay more attention to in order to navigate your entrepreneurial journey more effectively?

Conclusion

As we come to the end of this book, I want to express my deep gratitude to you for accompanying me on this transformative journey. *The Human Entrepreneur* is not just a title but a philosophy we have explored through each chapter, highlighting how deeply personal and uniquely human the entrepreneurial journey can be.

Together, we have navigated the wisdom of identifying your core values, strengths, and passions and how these personal attributes shape your business endeavors. We have delved into the art of crafting a brand that resonates on a human level, tackled the emotional highs and lows of entrepreneurship, and equipped ourselves with strategies for sustainable growth and resilience.

My hope for you, as you read the final page, is that you feel a renewed sense of purpose and readiness. This book was designed to empower you with not just knowledge but also the wisdom to use that knowledge in ways that honor your individuality as an entrepreneur. Your journey doesn't end here; it's just beginning, and the paths you choose now are full of potential for personal and professional fulfillment.

The world needs more than just businesses; it needs businesses that embody the human spirit, businesses that reflect their creators' strengths and values. As you move forward, I encourage you to continue embracing the essence of being a **Human Entrepreneur**, blending your humanity with your entrepreneurial spirit to create ventures that make a meaningful impact.

I invite you to join our community at www.thehumanentrepreneur.co, where we continue to support, inspire, and learn from one another. Here, you can find further resources, engage with peers, and explore how our advanced courses and personalized coaching can further your entrepreneurial journey.

Thank you for sharing this journey with me. The concept of *The Human Entrepreneur* is not just a perspective but a movement. Let us keep pushing the boundaries of what it means to be an entrepreneur in a world that craves genuine human connection and innovation.

We would love to see photos of you reading the book or applying what you've learned. To share your story and experiences with *The Human Entrepreneur* on social media, use #HumanEntrepreneur.

Join Our Community of Human Entrepreneurs

We would like to invite you to join our thriving community of aspiring entrepreneurs who are looking to start and grow their knowledge-based businesses. Our community is deeply rooted in the philosophy of the **Human Entrepreneur** and the **IdentityBrand Cycle**.

At **IdentityBrand**, we have helped more than two thousand people across the Middle East and beyond achieve their entrepreneurial dreams and launch successful brands over the past decade. We offer world-class training and renowned accelerator programs resulting in numerous stories of inspiration, growth, and success.

Our approach has been so effective that we have doubled our revenue since 2020. We endeavor to continue empowering passionate leaders to supercharge their businesses. Our success is a testament to the profound impact of aligning business endeavors with human values.

If you are ready to take the next step and join a community that values human-centered entrepreneurship, please visit our website at www.thehumanentrepreneur.co. There, you'll find a survey to help you identify which products or services best align with your aspirations and how you can start your journey with us.

Thank you for considering this invitation to join our community. We believe that your future as a **Human Entrepreneur** is bright and together, we can achieve extraordinary things. Let's continue to inspire, innovate, and influence the business world with integrity and a deep connection to our shared human values.

A Final Gift: Questions to Fuel Your Heart

I would like to offer you a personal toolkit. These are the ten questions that have had a profound impact on my mindset. I have gathered them from various sources over the years and turn to them whenever I feel lost or need to realign my path. These questions are designed to challenge your current thinking, spark deep introspection, and guide you toward more intentional actions:

1. What can I do to make my life more meaningful?
2. If I repeat this week's actions for ten years, where will it lead, and is that where I want to be?
3. What is the economic value of my hour?
4. What would my life look like over the next five years if money wasn't an issue and I could do whatever I wanted?
5. How can I show my love and care to my family and friends in addition to my ideal customers?
6. Why do I do what I do?
7. What was today's biggest win, and why?
8. Do I own my business, or does my business own me?
9. What are my most rewarding habits, financially and emotionally?
10. What would I like people to say at my funeral?

As you ponder these questions, remember that the journey of self-discovery and entrepreneurship is continuous. Each question is a stepping stone to deeper understanding and greater achievements. I encourage you to revisit them regularly as part of your reflective practice.

Now, as you step forward, energized by the possibilities that lie ahead, remember that our community at **IdentityBrand** is here to support you. Visit our website, join our programs, and start your journey to becoming a **Human Entrepreneur** who not only dreams but acts with conviction and purpose.

THANK YOU FOR READING MY BOOK!

DOWNLOAD YOUR FREE GIFTS

Just to say thanks for buying and reading my book, I would like to give a free welcome call with me, no strings attached!

Scan the QR Code:

SCAN ME

I appreciate your interest in my book, and value your feedback as it helps me improve future versions of this book. I would appreciate it if you could leave your invaluable review on Amazon.com with your feedback. Thank you!

Made in the USA
Columbia, SC
11 November 2024

f621ea7f-a613-478b-9205-c53e4d7c92f4R01